ALCOHOL POLICIES AND PRACTICES ON COLLEGE AND UNIVERSITY CAMPUSES

DAT*

**Edited by
Joan Sargent Sherwood
Assistant to the President
Western Washington University**

Volume 7; NASPA Monograph Series
Published by the National Association
of Student Personnel Administrators, Inc.

I

Library of Congress Cataloging-in-Publication Data
Alcohol policies and practices on college and university campuses edited by Joan Sargent Sherwood.
    p. cm. — (NASPA monograph series ; v. 7)
    Includes bibliographies.
    ISBN 0-931654-09-2 : $7.50
    1. College students — United States — Alcohol use. 2. Alcoholism — Study and teaching — United States. 3. Alcoholism — United States — Prevention. I. Sherwood, Joan Sargent, 1934- . II. Series.
LA229.A68 1987   362.2 '92' 088375—dc19   87-18442
                                                     CPI

ISBN-0-931654-09-2

II

NASPA Monograph Board 1986-87

Volume 7 Edited by 1986-87 Monograph Board

CONTRIBUTORS

ALAN D. BERKOWITZ is Clinical Psychologist and Co-Director (with H. Wesley Perkins) of the Alcohol Education Research Project at Hobart & William Smith Colleges, Geneva, New York.

RUTH C. ENGS is Associate Professor in the Department of Applied Health Sciences at Indiana University, Bloomington.

DAVID J. HANSON is Professor of Sociology and Coordinator of the Graduate Program in Human Services at the State University of New York's College of Arts and Science at Potsdam.

MARY LOU FENILI is Vice President and Dean for Student Life at Pacific Lutheran University in Tacoma, Washington.

JOSEPH M. FISCHER is Associate Director of Housing and Residential Life at Southern Oregon State College in Ashland, Oregon, and is working on a Doctor of Philosophy degree in Adult Education through Oregon State University with a research emphasis in the area of college student alcohol abuse and alcoholism.

GERARDO M. GONZALEZ is the founder of BACCHUS of the United States, Inc., the national college and community organization for the prevention of alcohol abuse, and currently serves as Associate Professor of Counselor Education at the University of Florida. He is also a private consultant in the field of alcohol, drug abuse, and health promotion.

TOM GOODALE is Vice Chancellor for Student Affairs and Professor of Education at the University of Denver.

H. WESLEY PERKINS is Associate Professor of Sociology and Co-Director (with Alan D. Berkowitz) of the Alcohol Education Research Project at Hobart & William Smith Colleges, Geneva, New York.

JOAN SARGENT SHERWOOD is serving as Assistant to the President at Western Washington University in Bellingham, Washington, where she is responsible for student development research projects.

CARYL K. SMITH is Associate Vice President for Student Affairs and Dean of Student Life at the University of Kansas in Lawrence, Kansas.

In memory of Jeffrey David Mohn

CONTENTS

PREFACE

In October 1984, Western Washington University experienced the loss of a student in an alcohol-related death. In response to that trauma, the Division of Student Affairs hired an alcohol consultant to look at the problem of alcohol abuse among college students at the university and to make recommendations for future actions. One of the results of the report issued by the consultant was the formation of a task force charged with making policy recommendations for the university. At the time of this writing, that task force is meeting regularly to deliberate these issues for the campus. A second result of the student's death has been the writing of this monograph, which began as a position paper for the National Association of Student Personnel Administrators and was expanded when it became apparent that the multifaceted problem of alcohol use and abuse on campus needed a more comprehensive examination. This monograph offers guidelines for colleges and universities across the country to examine and pursue.

I would like to extend a very special thanks to my secretary, Bobbie Coleman, and her assistants, Shirley Manuel, Linda Brown, Kathie Merrick, and Darlene Bloomfield. They worked diligently over the course of months to turn the preliminary drafts into a polished manuscript. Without their efforts, this task could not have been accomplished.

I am also grateful to Frederick R. Preston, Vice President at the State University of New York at Stony Brook and Chair of the Policy Issues Committee for the National Association of Student Personnel Administrators, for suggesting that the topic was worthy of a monograph, and to George Kuh, Editor of the *NASPA Monograph Series*, for his encouragement and support during the process. It is our intent that colleges and universities will use this monograph in their efforts to combat the problem of alcohol abuse on campus.

Joan Sargent Sherwood

Introduction

Tom Goodale

This monograph, initiated by the Policy Issues Committee of the National Association of Student Personnel Administrators, brings together members of the higher education community to address the issue of abuse of alcohol currently on our campuses. The authors address the issues of legal liability, university responses to changes in the legal drinking age, drinking patterns and problems of college students, and ways to combat alcohol abuse on the campus. This publication gives every college and university an opportunity to examine its role in responding to one of our nation's most serious social problems by providing information useful for designing a plan for alcohol policy implementation. The sharing of theories and observations, and even debate, are welcome and important in combating what has become one of America's major health problems. Only through concerted action can we begin to solve this very difficult problem that affects so many of our students and other members of the academic community.

Since Dr. Morris Chafetz, the first director of the National Institute on Alcoholism and Alcohol Abuse, developed a "University 50 Plus 12 Program" in 1973, a series of initiatives throughout the country have aimed to develop awareness and interventions in the area of campus alcohol abuse, particularly as it relates to students. More recently, BACCHUS (Boost Alcohol Consciousness Concerning the Health of University Students), a student organization with over 200 chapters in nearly every state in the nation and in Canada, initiated the "Inter-Association Task Force on Alcohol Issues." This Task Force, representing nearly all college administrators and student leaders involved in student affairs work in higher education, held a National Conference on Alcohol Policy on Campus to find areas of agreement among the diverse constituencies. The policies described in this monograph are from the Task Force and are an attempt to build a coalition between such regulatory agencies as the Alcohol and Beverage Control Agencies and the campuses to aid in the prevention of alcohol misuse and therefore to decrease risk liability—"an everyone wins" relationship. The message sent out with that consensus is exactly what will give a campaign the appeal and the urgency of an intense national movement—a bandwagon to be joined. If the community of national consensus is prepared to answer all vital questions about the alcohol abuse issue, whether it be funding, structure, resource management, legal fiat, or campus community and reinforcement, college presidents and other campus administrators can expect effective execution of policy and program initiatives. The writers relate realistically to what is currently underway on many campuses and to what needs to be done. They come from diverse sectors of the academic community including student affairs, legal counsel, social sciences, and the service professions. Their keen insight can give the reader the necessary supportive documentation to develop important dialogue on the campus.

In Chapter 1, Joe Fischer examines the abuse of alcohol in American higher education from a historical perspective. Of particular importance is his discussion of the hereditary and genetic nature of alcoholism, carefully distinguishing alcoholism from alcohol abuse by describing how the alcoholic metabolizes alcohol in a way different from the heavy drinker. He also discusses successful treatment modalities, reports recent research, and comments on current prevention models underway on campuses.

The pervasive nature of legal liability is presented by Mary Lou Fenili in Chapter 2. She uses case law and documentation from actual court decisions to illustrate the need for a risk management program for all institutions. The most important of these cases is *Bradshaw v. Rawlings*. Although the resolution of this case was favorable for colleges and universities in that the court did not find a custodial or special relationship between the institution and the student, Fenili cautions the reader against believing that the case protects the institution from liability. Only a few minor changes in the case could have reversed that decision. Fenili also examines the relationship of the institution to the fraternity/sorority system and specifically concentrates on statutes prohibiting hazing. Her overview is a practical resource for the chief student officer and college or university counsel.

In Chapter 3, Caryl Smith examines the federal legislation mandating the raise in drinking age and its impact on post-secondary education. She presents a model initiative (one taken by her own institution, the University of Kansas) to respond to the legislation, and then summarizes the impact of this legislation on small college campuses and a selected number of other campuses. Student responses to the changes and the implications for professional student affairs leadership are also discussed.

Empirical research data, so important as a foundation for the formulation of programs and policies, is reported by Drs. Engs and Hanson, noted scholars in the alcohol education field, in Chapter 4. Gender and ethnic demographics are presented as they relate to collegiate drinking practices. Specifically, Engs and Hanson outline the differences in beverage preference and drinking locations by gender and among black collegians, and then focus upon the drinking problems among men and women collegians, both black and white. This chapter gives us a clear picture of collegiate drinking practices, distinguishing between gender demographics and black and white racial demographics.

The uniqueness of an institution of higher learning and its special opportunity for cognitive enhancement are outlined by college faculty members Alan Berkowitz and Wes Perkins, research project directors. They introduce, in Chapter 5, a theoretical approach for evaluating alcohol program effectiveness, based on sociological principles that are useful in understanding the importance of a prevention program. They point out that the acquisition of knowledge rarely translates into positive behavioral change, although this does not indicate that the programs are ineffective. More recent strategies are focusing on peer influence as a means of changing drinking patterns, taking into consideration the social environment of the campus. Berkowitz and Perkins stress heavily the need to evaluate a program's effectiveness; they also provide strategies for assessing the changes made as a result of the introduction of alcohol programs.

In the final chapter, Gerardo Gonzalez, founder of a campus-based alcohol awareness and education program called BACCHUS, reviews methodology for policy initiatives. His evaluation of a public health model, the current issues in legal liability, and a suggested model institutional policy give a comprehensive outline for campus constituencies to examine and consider for their own implementation.

Recently the American Council on Education issued a white paper that addressed tort liability in alcohol abuse on college campuses. The conclusion presented therein is that *all* colleges and universities have alcohol policies, consisting of the actual practices of each school. The lack of a written policy on alcohol use leaves a "duty to care" void that invites litigation. At the other end of the continuum, if a college or university adopts strict rules and fails to enforce them, a judge or jury may find that the university failed to live up to its own standard of care. Schools can most readily defend their policies when the rules governing student drinking are realistic and consistently enforced. The paper goes on to state that the rules need to emphasize students' personal responsibility as an important component in campus alcohol policy. The Inter-Association Task Force created a policy model that specifically addresses the need for college and university administrations to have on record and to fully distribute campus-wide a policy that is comprehensive and realistic. In reading the position papers of the authors, it is important when thinking about a policy to ask these questions:

1. Does it go as far as it can?
2. Should it go further?
3. Does it document well-thought-out administrative awareness of concern?
4. Does it provide reasonable strategies in sound support systems?

Such a policy can assist in deciding where university responsibility *must* end and where student responsibility *must* begin. The policy cannot be merely filed away in a dean's office. It must also be enforced and visible. There must be an active structure—a means by which that policy is consistently promoted, reinforced, and evaluated. Someone has to be responsible for its daily maintenance. Until now, allocating those kinds of financial human resources was a major roadblock for many college and university presidents and their subordinates. Now, with the information contained in these papers and a strong commitment from a consensus, change must occur in students. Alcohol abuse among students can be lessened. A reasonable and realistic balance between the educational mission and the enforcement responsibilities of the institution must be sought. While rules and regulations are important and necessary, the reduction of problems related to the misuse of alcohol cannot be achieved solely through the development of rules and regulations; students must be educated about the principles behind the policies. Alcohol education should be as central to the curriculum as any course of study for individual and social skills development, business preparation, relationship management, decision making, and help in physical conditioning. Vigorously and consistently communicating a comprehensive alcohol program does much to satisfy an institution's "duty to care" responsibility. Clear-cut guidelines give students an understanding of how they may use their substantial peer influence in a positive manner. Positive campus leadership that promotes the dissemination of information on campuses fills a void for local legislators and law-enforcement agencies who so often react precipitously when a void exists. It enables them to work closely with lawmakers while avoiding passing reactionary laws that so often prove to be an overreaction to the problem.

In summary, this monograph hopefully will be a catalyst for thought and a useful document to those attempting to deal with the complicated problems created by alcohol abuse on campus. It provides information that can help to open lines of communication and initiate useful dialogue on campus. It suggests how to establish effective policies.

Chapter 1

A Historical Perspective: Alcohol Abuse and Alcoholism in America and on Our Campuses

Joseph M. Fischer

A Working Definition

A brief discussion of the difference between alcohol abuse and alcoholism is necessary for a complete understanding of the historical perspective of alcohol abuse and alcoholism. First, definitions are in order. Alcohol abuse and alcoholism are two similar, yet distinct, problems (Kinney & Leaton, 1983; Milam & Ketcham, 1983). Where alcohol abuse involves the abusive consumption of alcohol to deal with stress or other life problems, there is no physical addictive reaction to alcohol. Alcoholism, on the other hand, involves a physical addictive reaction by the body to alcohol. Although many of the behaviors exhibited by the alcohol abuser and the alcoholic are similar, the implications for education, intervention, and treatment are significantly different.

A workable definition of alcoholism for student affairs professionals, and one accepted by many professionals in the alcohol field, is proposed by Kinney and Leaton (1983): "Alcoholism is a physical, chronic, progressive disease in which the person's use of alcohol *continues* despite problems it causes in any area of life" (p.50). This definition emphasizes the disease concept of alcoholism, the lack of control involved in alcohol consumption, the problem-causing nature of the disease, and the dependency on alcohol.

The definition for alcohol abuse is only slightly different than that for alcoholism. Drawing the fine line between the two concepts is often difficult, but doing so is necessary in order for student affairs professionals to understand why certain types of alcohol education programs and alcohol policies have not effectively addressed the problems associated with college student alcoholism. The best way to define alcohol abuse is to describe the differences between alcohol abuse and alcoholism. A student who abuses alcohol does not develop a tolerance for the drug; he/she does not develop a physically addictive reaction to the drug; he/she will more than likely discontinue abusive drinking when the problems caused by such drinking become significant. But, as demonstrated by the definition of alcoholism, the student alcoholic is physically addicted to alcohol and cannot stop drinking abusively despite life problems. Still, there is no clear criterion for the early differentiation between alcoholism and alcohol abuse, and many use the term *alcohol abuse* to make the problem more palatable to society because the word *alcoholism* is still loaded with emotional and moral overtones (Kinney & Leaton, 1983).

A working definition for the student affairs professional would include the recognition of any problems caused by the student's consumption of alcohol that affect the student's academic career. These problems could include interpersonal problems, inappropriate behavior, health problems, and so forth. Thus, the student affairs professional might work with the following definition: Student alcohol abuse is present when the student's continued use of alcohol creates problems for the student in any part of his/her academic career. This working definition allows colleges and universities to address the problem in terms of the student's academic career and disregards any moral or personal value judgments. If actual alcoholism is suspected, the earlier definition offered by Kinney and Leaton (1983) should be considered and applied to a student's specific situation.

The Scope of the Problem

Belohlav and Popp (1983) cite statistics from the Bureau of National Affairs indicating that substance abuse on a national level, including alcoholism and alcohol abuse, is reaching "epidemic proportions." Currently 70% of adult Americans are regular users of alcohol. This percentage increases to 90% for teens between the ages of 17 and 19. Estimates of the number of drinking Americans suffering from alcoholism range from 8% to 15%, while an even greater percentage of the drinking population suffer from some type of alcohol abuse at one time or another (Kinney & Leaton, 1983; Milam & Ketcham, 1983; Olson & Gerstein, 1985). Pati and Adkins (1983) conclude that, "in the U.S., alcoholism is exceeded in frequency only by mental illness and cardiovascular disease." The influence of alcoholism and alcohol abuse is not confined to just the drinking individual. Alcoholism has been classified as a family disease in that the disruption created in the alcoholic's life seriously affects the lives of at least four other people close to the drinking individual (Kinney & Leaton).

Still, the problems of alcohol abuse and alcoholism show no signs of slowing down among our nation's youth (National Institute on Drug Abuse, 1986; Olson & Gerstein, 1985). Rather, as mentioned earlier, these problems are assuming epidemic proportions in America and are increasing more rapidly among college students than among other groups of young people (Johnston, O'Malley, & Bachman, 1986).

Historical Responses to Alcohol Abuse and Alcoholism

The problems associated with alcohol abuse have existed since before the beginning of our nation. The following summary, taken mostly from the excellent reference work by Kinney and Leaton (1983), should provide a basic framework for understanding what these problems were and how we responded to them.

The first organized responses to alcohol abuse began in the 1800s. These responses took the form of temperance movements, which began as the result of a rise in social consciousness regarding abusive drinking and its resulting behaviors (Moore & Gerstein, 1981). Later, all use of alcohol became a major concern, and the influence of religious and political factions moved the temperance movement from a rehabilitative orientation to a condemning orientation emphasizing that any consumption of alcohol was a moral weakness and a sin. The strength of the temperance movement finally resulted in Congress's passing of the Eighteenth Amendment—officially called the Volstad Act—in 1919, which prohibited the manufacture, distribution, and sale of alcoholic beverages. Thus, prohibition began, and it lasted from 1920 until 1933.

After prohibition efforts failed, new responses to alcohol abuse and alcoholism began to focus on assisting individuals with problems. The National Council on Alcoholism was founded in 1944 by Dr. E. M. Jellinek, an alcohol researcher from Yale University, and Marty Mann, a recovering alcoholic. In 1971, the National Institute on Alcohol Abuse and Alcoholism (NIAAA) was founded to sponsor research, public education, and treatment programs for alcoholism and alcohol abuse. The NIAAA was made possible by landmark legislation passed by Congress in 1970. This bill was officially titled "The Comprehensive Alcohol Abuse and Alcoholism Prevention, Treatment and Rehabilitation Act." In the past 15 years, several efforts have been undertaken by the government to respond to the problems of alcohol abuse and alcoholism in the United States. A continuing debate surrounds efforts to pass the Uniform Alcoholism and Intoxication Treatment Act, which would provide a universal way of responding to public intoxication across all 50 states. Also, Congress has passed numerous bills providing funding for research in the areas of substance abuse, education, and treatment.

Attitudes About Alcohol Abuse and Alcoholism

In examining the response to alcoholism and alcohol abuse in the United States over the last 150 years, it seems that social attitudes about alcohol abuse and alcoholism have evolved through three basic views (Kinney & Leaton, 1983). The first view of alcohol abuse and alcoholism was the attitude that these problems represented a moral weakness or a lack of willpower in the individual experiencing these problems. These people were sinners and should be punished for their drunkenness. This attitude still persists today to a great degree in our society and is based on myths and a lack of knowledge concerning alcohol abuse and alcoholism.

The second view, which began to surface in the early 1900s, focused on alcoholism and alcohol abuse as a psychological illness caused by a combination of the individual's personality makeup, his/her environment while growing up, and current environmental factors, such as stress. Basically, this view proposed that psychological problems caused alcoholism and that successful treatment of alcoholism must first start with treating the patient's psychological problems. While this view might be appropriate as an explanation for alcohol abuse, it is not a good explanation for the causes of alcoholism. It is probable that this view, along with the first, significantly retarded research into the metabolic factors of alcoholism.

The third, and the most current and accepted view in the alcohol field, is that alcoholism is a physical illness that results in psychological and other problems. Current research has dispelled most of the old myths about alcoholism. Although there may still be influences from a combination of environmental and psychological factors, the predominant cause of alcoholism is the way the body metabolizes alcohol. Also, current research seems to suggest that the way the body metabolizes alcohol is inherited, thus suggesting that alcoholism might be a hereditary disease similar to diabetes or epilepsy. As research progresses in the alcohol field, this view is gaining more support and credibility.

The Hereditary and Genetic Nature of Alcoholism

Knowledge of the disease concept of alcoholism is necessary for student affairs professionals to understand why higher education's traditional efforts of education and discipline in addressing student alcohol problems have not proven effective for a large proportion of students. If 10% to 15% of college students are "genetically predisposed" to become alcoholics if they drink, if more than 90% of college students drink alcohol, and if these students start their drinking in grade school or junior high school, then a large proportion of students on our campuses drinks addictively. Thus, a strictly disciplinary orientation to college student alcohol problems precludes the development and implementation of effective and efficient programs to address these problems.

Jellinek's famous 1944 book entitled *The Disease Concept of Alcoholism*, along with the recognition of alcoholism as a disease by the American Medical Association and other professional organizations, prompted rigorous research efforts in the area of alcohol abuse and alcoholism. This research has further supported the disease concept of alcoholism. In order to better understand the disease concept of alcoholism, it is helpful to briefly discuss three interrelated areas of research in the alcohol field: heredity, metabolism, and genetics.

Research into the hereditary aspect of alcoholism has produced consistent results. Accumulated evidence clearly indicates that alcoholism is hereditary. "Physiology, not psychology, determines whether one drinker will become addicted to alcohol and another will not" (Milam & Ketcham, 1983, p. 34). Most professionals in the alcohol field will agree that a person has a one-in-two chance of becoming an alcoholic if one of his/her biological parents was alcoholic, and an even greater chance if both biological parents were alcoholic (Kinney & Leaton, 1983; Milam & Ketcham, 1983). These probabilities for becoming alcoholic are significantly higher than those for individuals whose biological parents were not alcoholic.

Research conducted by Dr. Donald Goodwin, and cited in both Kinney and Leaton (1983) and Milam and Ketcham (1983), provides strong support for the hereditary nature of alcoholism. Goodwin performed several twin and adoption studies in attempts to separate environmental influences from hereditary influences in the cause of alcoholism. His research consistently found that children of alcoholic biological parents had a much higher risk of developing the disease, despite their environment while growing up. Similarly, children of nonalcoholic biological parents had a much lower risk of developing alcoholism, even when raised by alcoholic foster parents. Goodwin also compared the children of alcoholic and nonalcoholic biological parents for psychiatric problems and found that these two groups were "virtually indistinguishable." Thus, Goodwin found more evidence to support the theory that alcoholism is a hereditary disease.

Some research on hereditary influences has also been performed with college students. Ronald G. Thurman, a professor of pharmacology at the University of North Carolina at Chapel Hill, found a relationship between the rate that male college students metabolized alcohol and the incidence of self-reported problems with alcohol experienced by the students and their immediate families (Staff, 1984, May 23).

The hereditary basis for the disease of alcoholism is found in the way alcohol is metabolized in the body. Research continues to support the theory that the alcoholic and nonalcoholic metabolize alcohol in different ways and that this metabolic difference may be the key to why someone becomes alcoholic (Kinney & Leaton, 1983; Milam & Ketcham, 1983). Milam and Ketcham cite research conducted at the University of California at San Diego that demonstrates the key differences in the metabolism of alcohol in alcoholic and nonalcoholic individuals. The nonalcoholic transforms alcohol into acetaldehyde in the liver by the interaction of alcohol with several liver enzymes. This acetaldehyde is then turned into acetic acid, which in turn is transformed into carbon dioxide and water, and is passed from the body. The alcoholic seems to have a different combination of certain liver enzymes, which results in a much slower metabolism of acetaldehyde. This results in a buildup of certain enzymes and a suppression of other enzymes, which in turn increase the buildup of amines in the brain. These amines are the molecules that transmit neurological impulses in the brain. The brain also experiences an imbalance of compounds called isoquinolines, the most influential of which is tetrahydraisoquinoline (THIQ). Isoquinolines are very much like opiates, and researchers believe that the THIQ, along with other isoquinolines, may act upon the opiate receptors of the brain, causing an addictive reaction to alcohol.

Studies of alcoholics' children who had never consumed an alcoholic beverage showed that they experienced the same metabolic problems as a drinking alcoholic when converting acetaldehyde into acetic acid. Thus, it seems that the alcoholic is hereditarily predisposed to the disease even before he/she ever starts drinking. This is a somewhat simplified explanation of the metabolic process that takes place in the alcoholic's body, but it does provide a strong and persuasive explanation of the possible reasons why alcoholism is an inherited disease.

Research in the hereditary and metabolic areas of alcoholism have led to the postulation of the "genetic marker" theory (Kinney & Leaton, 1983). This theory suggests that there is a genetic structure that is common among alcoholics, as well as one among nonalcoholics, which determines how the body will metabolize alcohol. This seems to be consistent with the idea that alcoholism is hereditary, and a great many professionals in the alcohol field support this theory. If the specific genetic pattern or patterns that cause alcoholism can be isolated, then it would be possible to test individuals for a predisposition to developing alcoholism if they drink alcohol. This theory also further differentiates between alcoholism and alcohol abuse. The alcohol abuser would not show the genetic pattern that might result in addiction to alcohol and could be treated appropriately. The person who has the genetic pattern that indicates predisposition to alcohol addiction could be treated differently from the alcohol abuser, with more appropriate and timely methods.

Current Approaches to the Treatment of Alcohol Abuse and Alcoholism

Most treatment approaches for alcoholism and alcohol abuse in the United States incorporate a multifaceted approach. Currently, it is hard to differentiate between alcohol abuse and alcoholism. Consequently, until it can be determined whether an individual is suffering only from alcohol abuse or from the disease of alcoholism, most treatment programs approach both problems in the same way.

The initial approach to dealing with serious alcohol problems involves three aspects. First, it is important to accept the fact that the disease of alcoholism is physical and as such requires complete abstinence from alcohol. Second, medical attention (including nutrition) is a key component in assisting the individual suffering from alcoholism in regaining a metabolic balance within him/herself. Third, the alcoholic must receive psychological counseling and support to help deal with the inappropriate and disruptive behaviors that have developed as a response to the addictive use of alcohol (Kinney & Leaton, 1983; Zimberg, Wallace, & Blume, 1978).

Currently, there is no universal knowledge base regarding alcoholism treatment. "The problem is not a lack of knowledge, but the fact that this knowledge is scattered all over the landscape of the various life sciences. What is needed is not more isolated facts and information but a truly unifying scientific view of alcoholism" (Milam & Ketcham, 1983, p. 10). Criticism has been directed toward medical schools in the training of physicians, seminaries in the training of ministers, and toward other professional schools as well. It has been suggested that little time is devoted to these topics and that insufficient information is given to these young professionals to enable them to deal effectively with alcohol abuse problems and alcoholism. The field of alcoholism and alcohol problem resolution is becoming a specialized field, just as many medical and psychological fields have emerged from the general study of medicine and psychology. Hopefully, greater specialization of this field will lead to more effective treatment of alcoholism and alcohol abuse.

History of College and University Responses to Student Alcohol Abuse and Alcoholism

Before the 1960s, not much was done to deal effectively with college and university students' alcohol abuse and alcoholism. The typical reaction to problems resulting from alcohol abuse was probably a scolding from the dean and some type of disciplinary action. (This response is not uncommon in many colleges and universities, even today.) As concern grew regarding student drug use in the sixties and early seventies, so too did concern regarding students' use and abuse of alcohol, and this alcohol use and abuse became a separate and significant issue on campus. Some basic alcohol education programs were established on some campuses. However, most campuses were still working with the disciplinary approach, even into the mid-seventies.

The first organized attempt of any size to evaluate the status of colleges' and universities' approaches to student alcohol abuse and alcoholism was the University 50 + 12 project performed by the National Institute on Alcohol Abuse and Alcoholism during the 1974-75 academic year. This study examined 50 higher education institutions, one from each state, and 12 minority and private institutions. The goals of this program were to gather information about student drinking as well as colleges' and universities' responses to drinking; to disseminate information regarding alcohol, its use, and its abuse; and to focus attention on the problems of student alcohol abuse and encourage establishment of programs to address these problems (Hewitt, 1977). The findings of the 50 + 12 project, as summarized in Hewitt, include the fact that only 15% of the institutions in the study had any type of organized alcohol education program. Most of the rest of the institutions surveyed were interested in establishing programs but wanted guidance on what to do and how to do it. Most institutions recognized that student alcohol abuse was a problem, one that was often hidden. Alcohol problems were found to be the most prevalent in the residence halls. (This was probably because the institutions could monitor the behavior of students in the residence halls more easily than they could monitor the behavior of students who lived off-campus or student behavior in the classroom, library, or other parts of the campus.) Moderate to heavy drinking seemed to be common among college students, and the attitude or belief that getting drunk was OK or acceptable was extremely common. The results of the 50 + 12 project showed an immediate and definite need for programs to address the problems of student alcohol abuse on college and university campuses.

Hewitt (1977) summarizes the 1971 presentation by Jessor and Jessor, at that time of the University of Colorado, of the results of their study that confirmed the significant and universal use and abuse of alcohol by college students. Jessor and Jessor estimated that almost one-third of college students experienced drinking problems. They recommended a multifaceted approach to addressing these problems and to teaching students how to drink responsibly (Hewitt).

Campuses have been concerned about student alcohol use and abuse and have developed and implemented new policies and programs since the 50 + 12 project was completed. Significant changes have been made in policies regarding the serving of alcoholic beverages on campuses, requiring the serving of food and alternative beverages, and more regulation regarding advertising and regulation of the locations on campus where alcohol can be served (Anderson & Gadaleto, 1984). Also, the number of campuses that offer alcohol support groups for students, training of paraprofessional staff, and alcohol education and prevention programs has increased (Anderson & Gadaleto, 1986).

One of the most significant efforts to address the concern about student alcohol abuse and alcoholism on college and university campuses has been the joint effort of the National Association of Student Personnel Administrators (NASPA), the Association of College and University Housing Officers—International (ACUHO-I), the American College Personnel Association (ACPA), the United States Student Association (USSA), and the student organization to Boost Alcohol Consciousness Concerning the Health of University Students (BACCHUS) (Staff, 1984, August-September). In 1982 these five organizations, along with several other higher education organizations, formed the Inter-Association Task Force on Alcohol Issues to promote and coordinate efforts designed to bring attention to the problems of student alcohol abuse and to develop and implement individual campus educational programs in order to address these problems effectively. One example of their effort is the establishment of the National Collegiate Alcohol Awareness Week, which is sponsored during the second week of October every year. The coalition of these five organizations clearly demonstrates the serious concern about the significant problems of student alcohol abuse and alcoholism on college and university campuses today.

The public stand taken by Secretary of Education William J. Bennett, when he called on college presidents to crack down on student drug use (Meyer, 1986, July 16), represents one of the most recent efforts to address alcohol and drug problems on college campuses. Secretary Bennett's comments followed the drug-related deaths of several college athletes. He suggested that federal money might be withheld from colleges that do not mount efforts to combat drug abuse among students. Three months later, the House of Representatives voted to withhold federal funds from colleges or universities that did not have programs to fight student drug abuse (Palmer, 1986). Even though the wording of the statements by Secretary Bennett and the House of Representatives focused on "drugs," it would seem that there is an implicit meaning focused on the use and abuse of all drugs, including alcohol, which is the most used and abused drug on college campuses.

Secretary Bennett's plan has come under fire from college administrators as being naive and simplistic. Student affairs administrators indicate that colleges and universities have been aware of the abuse of drugs and alcohol among college students for years and that programs and regulations have been in place on campuses to address this problem (Meyer, 1986, July 23).

College and University Alcohol Programs

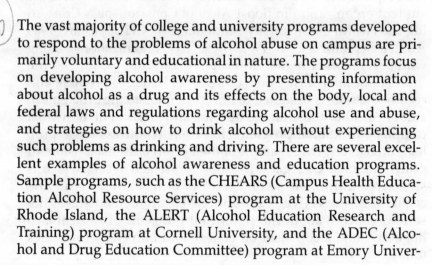

The vast majority of college and university programs developed to respond to the problems of alcohol abuse on campus are primarily voluntary and educational in nature. The programs focus on developing alcohol awareness by presenting information about alcohol as a drug and its effects on the body, local and federal laws and regulations regarding alcohol use and abuse, and strategies on how to drink alcohol without experiencing such problems as drinking and driving. There are several excellent examples of alcohol awareness and education programs. Sample programs, such as the CHEARS (Campus Health Education Alcohol Resource Services) program at the University of Rhode Island, the ALERT (Alcohol Education Research and Training) program at Cornell University, and the ADEC (Alcohol and Drug Education Committee) program at Emory University, are characteristic of alcohol education and awareness programs at colleges and universities today (Korde & Matzko, 1985).

Although education and awareness are currently the main focus of most alcohol programs on campuses, a variety of approaches have been used. Examples include voluntary and mandatory alcohol education seminars, credit classes on alcohol, peer counseling, professional counseling, values clarification workshops, residence hall staff training, student and faculty training, and referral to professional drug and alcohol counseling and treatment facilities, as well as other creative approaches to dealing with alcohol problems (Anderson & Gadaleto, 1984; Hewitt, 1977; Korde & Matzko, 1985; Rice, no publication date).

In reviewing the literature, it seems that the most common educational approach to alcohol awareness and programming focuses on information sharing intended to foster "responsible drinking" attitudes and behaviors. The "responsible drinking" approach to alcohol education is usually composed of the following major components: First, information is disseminated through voluntary programs often sponsored through the residence hall system or student government, as well as by student services offices. This information usually focuses on explaining what alcohol is, what effects it has on the body, and what constitutes responsible social drinking behaviors. Second, pamphlets, flyers, or small resource books are disseminated that provide much of the information described above. These documents are a means of reaching those students who do not avail themselves of the program offerings. A third major component is student input in the development, implementation, and evaluation of these programs. This grassroots student involvement seems to be essential for these types of programs to experience any type of long-term success. A fourth component is information gathering regarding alcohol use and abuse among students on campus. This may take the form of a simple questionnaire, or a psychometrically sophisticated instrument. The purpose is to gather information to provide direction for the program on a particular campus. These four components seem to be common in most alcohol education and awareness programs.

The "responsible drinking" approach to alcohol awareness and educational programming has gained much popularity since the establishment of BACCHUS (Ingalls, 1986). The "responsible drinking" approach focuses on assisting students to make informed decisions about their alcohol use, instead of moralizing about the issue of alcohol use and misuse. Students are encouraged to learn all they can about alcohol and its use, to determine if and how they will use alcohol, and then to learn, with assistance, how to use alcohol in a responsible manner that avoids problems for them and others. This approach also stresses that it is OK not to use alcohol and assists students in developing coping strategies if they choose not to drink.

There has been criticism of the "responsible drinking" approach. Howard T. Blane, Director of The Research Institute on Alcoholism, which is affiliated with the State University of New York at Buffalo, has criticized current alcohol education programs on college campuses as being too "broad-brush" and not effecting behavior changes that reduce alcohol abuse. He emphasizes that alcohol programming efforts should be targeted more toward groups of students who are in high-risk categories for developing alcohol problems, rather than trying to approach all students (Ingalls, 1984). Despite criticism, "responsible drinking" is still one of the most popular approaches to alcohol education and awareness programming.

Although the "responsible drinking" approach to alcohol programs is still the most prevalent on campuses, a growing minority of campuses are incorporating primary and secondary prevention efforts (Ingalls, 1984). Professionals in the alcohol field view primary prevention as focusing educational efforts concerning alcohol abuse and alcoholism toward people who have a high risk of developing problems with alcohol, usually children of alcoholics or individuals with alcoholism in their biological families. Secondary prevention efforts are regarded as intervention, i.e., trying to get someone who is having a problem with alcohol into some type of professional counseling or treatment program. Examples of these primary and secondary approaches are in effect at the University of California at Santa Barbara and at the University of Massachusetts at Amherst. As alcohol education and awareness programs grow, many will probably branch out to incorporate these primary and secondary approaches to dealing with alcohol abuse on college and university campuses.

Summary

Colleges and universities have experienced alcohol abuse and alcoholism problems among their students throughout the history of higher education. As colleges and universities represent a microcosm of society, college and university alcohol problems have followed the patterns of alcohol problems in American society. It seems that student alcohol abuse problems are growing. Institutions of higher education are beginning to recognize the scope of these problems and are addressing student alcohol abuse and alcoholism with organized educational programs. At this time, higher education has not implemented primary or secondary prevention methods in its approach to alcohol abuse, other than on a few isolated campuses. However, as college and university administrators become more knowledgeable about the hereditary-disease concept of alcoholism, responses to these problems will be more in line with successful state-of-the-art programs that address alcohol abuse and alcoholism. Higher education must address student alcohol abuse and alcoholism in more efficient and effective ways if the associated problems are to stabilize or subside.

References

Anderson, D. S., & Gadaleto, A. F. (1984, July). Progress or illusion: The 1979 and 1982 college alcohol surveys. *Journal of College Student Personnel*, pp. 332-337.

Anderson, D. S. & Gadaleto, A. F. (1986). *The college alcohol survey: 1979, 1982, and 1985.* Unpublished manuscript.

Belohlav, J., & Popp, P. O. (1983, July-August). Employee substance abuse: Epidemic of the eighties. *Business Horizons*, pp. 29-34.

Hewitt, K. (Ed.). (1977). *The whole college catalogue about drinking—a guide to alcohol abuse prevention.* Rockville, MD: U.S. Department of Health, Education, and Welfare.

Ingalls, Z. (1984, May 2). Campus programs called ineffective in ending student alcohol abuse. *The Chronicle of Higher Education,* p. 17.

Ingalls, Z. (1986, October 22). Alcohol-education pioneer toots up a decade of success. *The Chronicle of Higher Education,* p. 3.

Johnston, L., O'Malley, P., & Bachman, J. (1986). *Drug use among American high school students, college students, and other young adults.* (DHHS Publication No. ADM 86-1450). Washington, DC: U.S. Government Printing Office.

Kinney, J., & Leaton, G. (1983). *Loosening the grip: a handbook of alcohol information.* St. Louis, MO: The C.V. Mosby Company.

Korde, M., & Matzko, J. (Eds.). (1985). *American association of university students' universities' alcohol policies, programs and problems study.* (American Association of University Students).

Meyer, T. J. (1986, July 16). One in three college students tries cocaine, study finds; Bennett urges presidents to crack down on drugs. *The Chronicle of Higher Education,* p. 1.

Meyer, T. J. (1986, July 23). Colleges say Bennett's views on drugs ignore long-standing campus policies. *The Chronicle of Higher Education,* p. 23.

Milam, J.R., & Ketcham, K. (1983). *Under the influence: a guide to the myths and realities of alcoholism.* Seattle, WA: Madrona Publishers.

Moore, M. H., & Gerstein, D. R. (Eds.). (1981). *Alcohol and public policy: Beyond the shadow of prohibition.* Washington, DC: National Academy Press.

National Institute on Drug Abuse. (1986). *Drug use among American high school students, college students and other young adults* (DSHS Publication No. ADM 86-1450). Washington, DC: U.S. Government Printing Office.

Olson, S., & Gerstein, D. R. (1985). *Alcohol in America: Taking action to prevent abuse.* Washington, DC: National Academy Press.

Palmer, S. E. (1986, October 6). House votes to bar education-department funds from colleges that lack drug-abuse programs. *The Chronicle of Higher Education,* p. 1.

Pati, G., & Adkins, J.I., Jr. (1983). The employee's role in alcoholism assistance. *Personnel Journal,* 26 (7), pp. 568-572.

Rice, R.R. (Ed.). (No publication date). *A report on alcohol education and awareness programs for association of college and university housing officers—international.* (Association of College and University Housing Officers—International).

Staff (1984, August-September). Alcohol awareness efforts highlighted. *NASPA Forum,* Vol. 5, No. 1.

Staff (1984, May 23). Genetic link to alcoholism indicated by study. *The Chronicle of Higher Education,* pp. 5-8.

Zimberg, S., Wallace, J., & Blume, S. (1978). *Practical approaches to alcoholism psychotherapy.* New York, NY: Plenum Press.

Chapter 2

Learning, Libation, Liability

Mary Lou Fenili

Introduction

The ACE White Paper on Student Alcohol Abuse (Gulland and Flournoy, 1985) cogently states the cold, hard facts facing higher education in a society that has become exceedingly litigious and has taken a "get tough" posture toward alcohol abuse, especially by young people and by those who drink and drive. The white paper focuses on four functions common to colleges and universities that, plaintiffs may assert, impose alcohol-related duties of care on the college: the college as limited supervisor of student conduct, as property owner, as seller of alcohol, and as "social host." The white paper reviews recent cases that set forth the standards courts are applying to determine whether a duty of care exists in each function, and discusses the facts in cases in which courts have imposed liability on a college.

The white paper offers suggestions to help higher educational institutions confront and address many of the challenges student alcohol abuse presents. It is well-written, understandable to those not trained in the law, and a fine presentation of the major issues that are faced in the course of student affairs work. The white paper was not intended to be exhaustive on the subject. Additional aspects of the alcohol-abuse situation need attention: custodial relationships, the legal relationship between a fraternity/sorority and the institution, hazing, and institutional liability. It is these aspects that this paper addresses.

Caveat Lector

Legislative enactments and court decisions between the time of writing and the time of publication may have affected what is written here. The reader is urged to confer with competent counsel before taking any action.

Dram Shop Acts

All states impose *criminal* liability on licensed vendors who serve alcoholic beverages to certain specified persons or under certain specified conditions. Such criminal liability is part of each state's general scheme for regulating the sale of alcoholic beverages and reflects the general principle that licensure is a privilege rather than a right. The penalties for criminal liability include loss of license, fine, imprisonment, or some combination of the three.

Some states additionally impose *civil* liability in tort on certain persons who "provide" alcoholic beverages to specified classes of persons who subsequently cause injury or damage to third parties. Statutes imposing this civil liability are known as "dram shop acts" or "civil damage acts." The nature of dram shop acts varies considerably among the states that have enacted them. Who does the serving and who is served are the basic distinctions drawn. Tables 2.1 and 2.2 summarize these distinctions. The list of states provided here is not necessarily exhaustive, given the fluid nature of legislative action regarding alcoholic beverages.

A troublesome quirk! Illinois, Maine, and Vermont dram shop acts impose civil liability on the owner of the building in which alcoholic beverages are "inappropriately" sold. This statutory language presents troublesome possibilities for those institutions that own the houses occupied by fraternities and sororities and for those institutions that think they may have

Table 2.1
Liability Based on the Server

| | Person Who Serves | | |
State	Vendor	Seller, Furnisher, Giver	Social Hosts[1]
Alabama		X	Possibly
Alaska	X		
Arizona	X		
California		X	No
Colorado		X	Possibly
Connecticut	X		
District of Columbia	X		
Florida		X	Possibly
Georgia		X	Possibly
Idaho		X	
Illinois	X		No
Indiana		X	
Iowa	X		No
Louisiana		X	
Maine	X	X	Possibly
Massachusetts	X		
Michigan	X		No
Minnesota	X		
Missouri	X		No
New Mexico	X		X[2]
New York	X		
North Dakota		X	Possibly
Ohio		X	Possibly
Oregon	X		X[3]
Pennsylvania	X		
Rhode Island	X		No
Tennessee	X		
Utah		X	Possibly
Vermont		X	Possibly
Wyoming		X	Possibly

[1] The use of "furnishing" and/or "giving" *could* mean that the statute includes social-host liability. Institutions should review local case law to determine if and how the courts in a particular state have interpreted these terms for purposes of imposing civil liability.

[2] Alcoholic beverages are provided in reckless disregard of the rights of others.

[3] If serve visibly intoxicated person.

Table 2.2
Liability Based on Identity of Person Served

State	Person Served Anyone Who Becomes Intoxicated	A Minor Who Becomes Intoxicated	Intoxicated Person	Intoxicated Minor	Habitual Drunkard[3]
Alabama	X				
Alaska		X	X		
Arizona		X	X	X	
California			X[2]		
Colorado					X
Connecticut			X		
District of Columbia			X		
Florida		X			X
Georgia		X			
Idaho		X	X		
Illinois	X				
Indiana			X		
Iowa			X		
Louisiana					X
Maine		X	X		
Massachusetts		X	X		
Michigan			X		
Minnesota	X				
Missouri		X	X		
New Mexico		X	X	X	
New York			X		
North Dakota	X				
Ohio	X				
Oregon		X[1]	X		
Pennsylvania			X		
Rhode Island		X	X		
Tennessee		X	X		
Utah	X				
Vermont	X				
Wyoming		X			X

Note: Liability occurs only if the person served causes injury or damage as a result of intoxication.
[1] Only if a reasonable person would have requested identification from the minor or would have known the minor's identification was fraudulent.
[2] Obviously intoxicated minor.
[3] Requires a specified relative of the habitual drunkard to have provided prior written notice of the habitual drunkenness to the server.

shielded themselves from liability by contracting with an independent party to run their campus pubs.

Suppose that a sorority/fraternity decides to participate actively in a campus program aimed at reducing alcohol abuse. As part of that program, the sorority/fraternity decides to sell alcoholic beverages, rather than offering them free-flowing, at their social functions. The logic to this approach is appealing since it might very well reduce the consumption of alcoholic beverages at these functions. By obtaining a license to sell alcoholic beverages in their house owned by the institution, the sorority/fraternity exposes the institution to civil liability if a dram shop act should impose civil liability on the sorority/fraternity. A similar analysis applies to a campus pub operated by an independent contractor in an institution-owned facility.

Common Law Liability

In states that have not legislated civil liability for providing alcoholic beverages under prohibited circumstances, the courts may have used violation of criminal statutes against providing alcoholic beverages to certain individuals to find negligence and impose civil liability. This "common law" generally applies to vendors who provide alcoholic beverages to minors or intoxicated persons, but has in recent years also been extended to social hosts. A line of cases from New Jersey serves as the foundation for these rulings.

In *Rappaport v. Nichols* (1959), the court held a tavern owner liable for the death of the victim of a traffic accident caused by a minor who had been served by the tavern owner. The court determined that statutory prohibitions against sale of alcoholic beverages to minors and visibly intoxicated persons are for the protection of the general public. Therefore, the tavern owner had a duty to protect the interests of the "travelling public." The court found that the unreasonable risk of harm to the travelling public was "particularly evident in current times when travelling by car to and from the tavern is so commonplace and accidents from drinking are so frequent" (p.8).

In *Soronen v. Olde Milford Inn, Inc.* (1966), the court extended its ruling to cover intoxicated adults where the tavern keeper knew or should have known of the adult's intoxicated state. Social hosts were swept into the net by *Linn v. Rand* (1976), in which the court believed the "forward-looking and far-reaching philosophy" of *Rappaport* should also apply to negligent social hosts who serve minors. In *Linn*, the host had served excessive amounts of alcoholic beverages to a visibly intoxicated minor who the host knew would thereafter drive a car. The court found the possibility of accident or injury "devastatingly apparent in view of the ever-increasing incidence of serious automobile accidents resulting from drunken driving" (p. 19). In *Figuly v. Knoll* (1982), the court ensnared social hosts who furnish alcoholic beverages to obviously intoxicated persons.

Bradshaw v. Rawlings

Bradshaw (1979) contains language that affirms the difficult position in which institutions find themselves today in relation to their students. While there is cause for optimism which that language brings to those in higher education, there is also cause for caution in relying too heavily on *Bradshaw* as a shield against liability. In *Bradshaw*, the court held the beer distributor liable for the injuries. The court found that the distributor "had reason to know that the majority of those who would be consuming the beer were underage" (p. 143)—the underage sophomore class president had ordered the beer, although someone of legal age signed for the delivery.

In holding the distributor liable, the court sent a message about the nature of licensure, the "deep pocket" theory, and the economic reality of the marketplace. Licensure to sell alcoholic beverages is a privilege that imposes certain responsibilities on the licensee. Failing to meet these responsibilities exposes the licensee to negative consequences. Under the "deep pocket" theory, the court imposed liability on the party that appeared better able to pay. The economic reality of the marketplace is such that one involved in commerce may pass on the costs of doing business to customers through pricing decisions.

The "deep pocket" theory that presently concerns higher education might have involved the institution in *Bradshaw* had there not been a "deeper" pocket in the case. In analyzing the facts of the case, the court focused on whether the institution had assumed a custodial relationship by adopting a rule prohibiting alcohol possession or consumption, or whether a special relationship existed as a matter of law requiring the institution to control the conduct of a student driving a vehicle off campus or to protect a student during transportation to and from off-campus activities. The court found neither a custodial relationship nor a special relationship.

However, the result might have been different had the beer distributor not been involved. Suppose that the beer had been purchased in cases from several liquor stores by individuals of legal age and that the vendors had no reason to know by whom the beer was to have been consumed. Had all the other facts been the same, the court might have taken any of four approaches to the case.

1. The court might have found "extensive institutional involvement" sufficient to impose liability on the institution. That the event was an annual sophomore class activity; that a faculty member served as advisor to the class, participated with class officers in planning the picnic, and cosigned checks used to purchase beer; that publicity flyers were printed by the college duplicating facility and were posted prominently on the campus could serve as facts to support the notion of "extensive institutional involvement."

2. The court might have found that the institution had sufficient "reason to know that the great majority of drinkers who would consume the beer were underage" (*Bradshaw*, 1979, p. 143) and that it had a duty not to tolerate at institutional functions illegal behavior of which it had prior knowledge. The faculty member's involvement as outlined above, the extensive publicity on campus, and the drawings of beer mugs on the publicity flyers all provide ample notice to the institution. Since the event was an annual function of one of the four chronological classes, it can be termed an institutional function. Since institutions are expected to comply with all applicable laws, prior knowledge of underage drinking under these circumstances would require the institution to take steps to ensure that widespread violations of law did not occur. Such steps might include requiring anyone desiring to obtain beer to show appropriate identification and

providing alternative nonalcoholic beverages for minors. Such steps *might* be sufficient for the institution to meet its burden.

3. The court might have found a special relationship or a custodial relationship. In a different social climate, such as exists today, the court might have determined that the circumstances not sufficient to establish such a relationship in 1979 (for an incident that occurred in 1975) were sufficient to establish such a relationship in 1987. In interpreting facts and balancing competing interests, the court could simply reach a different conclusion, which would be as easily supportable by the same facts as the conclusion that the court did reach.

4. The court might have found that a class picnic held in an outdoor location following extensive publicity is *public* conduct that institutions *can* supervise and regulate, rather than private conduct that institutions cannot supervise and regulate. The *Bradshaw* analysis relied heavily on the difficulty of supervising and regulating *private* conduct.

Given the current climate toward alcohol abuse and the specter of a "national drinking age," one of these results appears possible.

One other factor bears mentioning here. In *Bradshaw*, the faculty adviser did not attend the picnic. The faculty member's presence at the picnic *could* have made a difference in the court's determination about the existence of a custodial relationship. I am *not* suggesting that advisers stay away from activities. I merely emphasize that this entire area remains sufficiently uncertain to require careful thought and vigilance.

Custodial Relationships

A custodial relationship occurs when one is legally required to take custody of another person or when one voluntarily takes custody of another person in such a way that the person "in custody" cannot exercise self-protection or is exposed to others who may harm the person. The custodian is thereby required (has the duty) to control the conduct of others so that they do not intentionally harm the person or create an unreasonable risk of harm to the person. The custodian must know or have reason to know of their ability to control others' conduct and of the necessity and opportunity for exercising such control (Restatement of Torts 2d, 320). Failure to control the conduct of òthers would be a breach of duty for which the custodian would be held liable to tort for injuries to the person "in custody."

In 1983, Lambda Chi Alpha adopted *Standards for Chapter Excellence,* which contained several provisions addressing alcohol-related issues. Among those were discipline for social misconduct, misbehavior, alcohol or drug abuse (Standard 25D); compliance with state and local laws and college/university policies concerning alcohol/drugs (Standard 25D); avoidance of tasteless, insensitive, demeaning, or offensive parties (Standard 25F); de-emphasis of alcohol in programming and advertising (Standard 25G); and alternative beverages and food at all social functions (Standard 25H). If a fraternity or sorority adopts standards such as these, a custodial relationship is not likely to be established if the standards are actively enforced. If they are not actively enforced, courts might find a custodial relationship under an appropriate set of facts.

An issue to be faced is the impact of a "national drinking age" on institutions' relationships with their students. Whether this will be sufficient to establish custodial relationships remains to be seen.

Two Oregon cases involving fraternities are worth noting here. In one case, the court imposed liability on the fraternity but not on its individual members, while in the other, the court imposed liability on the individual members but not on the fraternity. In the first case, the court found a custodial relationship, but in the second case it did not.

In *Wiener v. Gamma Phi Chapter of Alpha Tau Omega* (1971), the fraternity had rented a dude ranch for a party at which alcohol was served to a minor who was driving guests on behalf of the fraternity. The minor had an accident and injured a passenger. The court held the fraternity liable for the injury in its role as host but did not hold the individual member of the fraternity who had purchased and delivered the alcoholic beverages to the dude ranch or the owner of the dude ranch liable. The court reasoned that the individual member had no control over the dispensation of the alcoholic beverages at the party and that the mere ownership of the facility rented by another created no duty on the part of the owner to supervise what transpired during the rental period. Rather, hosting the event placed the duty squarely on the fraternity (p. 22). The fraternity's status as host and its direct involvement in serving the alcoholic beverages to the minor were sufficient to create a duty of care for the breach of which it would be held liable (p. 23).

In *Stein v. Beta Rho Alumni Association, Inc.* (1982), a woman hired to entertain at a Christmas party at the fraternity's local chapter house was assaulted and injured. Alcoholic beverages had been served prior to her arrival at the party, and many of the members and pledges present were minors. The court refused to impose vicarious liability on the fraternity for either the negligent acts or the reckless, willful, and intentional torts of the fraternity officers and members (pp. 637-638). Applying the precedent set in *Wiener*, the court held the fraternity as owner of the house to have no duty to supervise the party (p. 638) but to be simply a landlord like the owner of the dude ranch (p. 637).

It is clear at this time that custodial relationships are established in some states whenever a licensed vendor violates the law (dram shop acts), generally by serving a minor or an intoxicated person who subsequently causes injury or damage. Two Nevada cases address alcohol consumption within the context of fraternity initiation. The fraternity was held liable for injury to the initiate in the first case but not in the second. The court found a custodial relationship in the first case but not in the second.

In *Davies v. Butler* (1979), an initiate to the Sundowners, a social "drinking club" at the University of Nevada-Reno, died during initiation that involved forced consumption of alcoholic beverages over a 48-hour period. In the final ceremony, the initiates were admonished to drink large quantities of alcoholic beverages, including 190 proof "Everclear," within a period of 20-30 minutes. During the course of a 40- to 50-mile ride in the bed of an open pickup truck after the final ceremony, the initiate was found to have stopped breathing. The initiate was pronounced dead at a hospital, where a second initiate was treated for alcohol poisoning and revived after having been discovered unconscious.

In its reasoning, the court found the club members' behavior in the initiation to be willful and wanton misconduct. The court found the club to be aware of the danger created by retention of large amounts of alcohol in the system, since an initiate had been hospitalized the previous year. The court found it reasonably foreseeable that putting bottles of alcoholic beverages to the lips of initiates and screaming at them to drink would result in their consuming inordinate amounts of alcoholic beverages very quickly (p. 611).

In *Bell v. Alpha Tau Omega Fraternity, Eta Epsilon Chapter* (1982), a minor initiate was injured when he fell off the fraternity house roof. Following initiation activities, the initiate became drunk after consuming beer and wine in the fraternity house over a five-hour period. He engaged in a variety of acting-out behaviors, including attempting to enter one member's room by climbing the steeply pitched roof. After scrambling up one side of the roof, he removed his shoes for better traction going down the other side. When he went too close to the edge of the roof, he fell.

The court refused to find that the fraternity's violation of the criminal prohibition against serving minors constituted negligence as a matter of law (p. 161). Under this set of facts, the court found that the fraternity and its members did not act in a manner that would "naturally or probably" cause the initiate to get drunk and fall off the roof (p. 163).

These two cases illustrate the distinctions that courts seem to be drawing when they consider the issue of custodial relationships and who has a duty to protect an inebriated individual.

In the Sundowners case, one can see that the forced consumption of alcoholic beverages deprived the initiates of their "normal power of self-protection" (Restatement of Torts 2d, 320). Since the club members had knowingly engaged in the conduct that led to the intoxication of the initiates and since the consumption of alcoholic beverages at the direction of the club members was required for initiation, the club thereby voluntarily took custody of the initiates and was responsible for any injury which befell them as a result of their intoxication (Restatement of Torts 2d, 320).

In *Bell*, the initiate was not forced to consume alcoholic beverages, so no custodial relationship was established by the minor's voluntary consumption of alcoholic beverages in the fraternity house.

Relationship of Institution to the Fraternity/Sorority System

The relationship between institutions and fraternities and sororities is often not particularly clear. This is not necessarily by design, but usually the result of inattention because clarity has not been required. However, the changing legislative and judicial treatment of alcohol use and abuse and the potential for institutional liability make it imperative for institutions to clarify the nature of these relationships.

In 1984, NASPA proposed a statement on the relationship between institutions and international fraternities. The statement included sections addressing philosophy and commitment, role and scope of the host institution and the fraternity chapter, establishment of new chapters, chapter integrity according to the mission of the institution and the fraternity, alumni/ae support, governance of the fraternity system, judicial procedures, and provision for a method of evaluation.

NASPA's hope was that the statement could be agreed upon and issued jointly by NASPA, NIC, and Panhellenic, among others. However, agreement could not be reached, and the statement was not adopted.

Such a policy statement would be a prudent addition to a college risk-management program. Institutions considering adopting such a policy statement should consult with competent counsel and ensure that the statement reflects factors unique to the campus, meets institutional needs, and complies with applicable state and local laws. An institution adopting such a policy must remember that it needs to enforce the policy actively.

Hazing

At least 18 states have enacted statutes prohibiting hazing. These statutes differ in the definition of hazing, persons who

Table 2.3
Definitions of Hazing

State	Creating risk of bodily injury or endangering health[1]	Attempting or threatening bodily injury[2]	Physical violence or bodily injury[3]	Danger or injury to mental health	Subject to ridicule, shame, disgrace, or humiliation[4]	Discouraging someone from remaining in school or causing them to leave school[5]	Aiding, allowing, encouraging, or promoting hazing[6]	Willfully acquiescing in or failing to report hazing[7]	Knowing, reckless, or intentional conduct[8]
Alabama	X	X	X	X			X	X	X
Arkansas		X	X	X	X	X	X	X	
California	X		X	X	X				
Florida	X	X	X	X					X
Illinois					X				
Kentucky	X		X	X					X
Louisiana	X								
Maine	X		X	X				X	X
Maryland	X								X
Massachusetts	X		X	X					X
New Jersey	X	X	X				X		X
N. Carolina		X	X		X		X		
Ohio	X		X	X	X				
Oregon	X	X	X	X			X		
Rhode Island	X	X	X	X	X				X
Texas	X	X	X		X	X		X	
Virginia			X						
Wisconsin	X		X						X

[1] This definition could encompass forced consumption of alcoholic beverages as it can lead to alcohol poisoning, which may render a person unconscious or endanger his/her health.

[2] Forced consumption could fit here as well, especially if someone physically restrains others in an effort to force them to drink.

[3] Alcohol poisoning could be sufficient bodily injury.

[4] Forced consumption of alcoholic beverages as a rite of initiation usually occurs under circumstances that make a spectacle of the initiate.

[5] A particularly humiliating initiation experience coupled with having to see regularly those present during the humiliation could cause someone to choose to leave rather than "relive" the experience.

[6] This covers those who are present during hazing, whether or not they actively participated, and active participants, however minor their role. A person who informs others that hazing is planned, even if that person does not otherwise participate, would be covered by this provision.

[7] This reaches those who are aware that hazing occurs and who tolerate it.

[8] Mere negligence is insufficient to be considered hazing, even if the conduct otherwise appears to fit the definition.

may be held liable for hazing, and the nature of the penalties for hazing. Tables 2.3, 2.4, and 2.5 summarize these statutes.

Florida, Massachusetts, Oregon, Rhode Island, and Wisconsin have adopted statutes that address problems already facing much of higher education. These statutes ban a variety of activities known to be used during fraternity initiation rites, many of which have already led to tragedies.

Florida prohibits forced calisthenics; exposure to the elements; forced consumption of food, liquor, drugs, or other substances; forced physical activity (other than competitive sports) that could adversely affect physical health and safety; or imposition of extreme mental stress such as sleep deprivation, forced exclusion from social contact, forced conduct that could result in extreme embarrassment, and forced activity that could adversely affect the mental health or dignity of the individual.

Oregon prohibits calisthenics; total or substantial nudity; compelled ingestion of any substance; wearing or carrying of any obscene or physically burdensome article; physical assaults or offensive physical contact; boxing matches or other physical contests (other than competitive sports); transportation and abandonment; confinement to unreasonably small, unventilated, unsanitary, or unlighted areas; assignment of pranks to be performed; and compelled personal servitude.

Massachusetts and Rhode Island prohibit whipping; beating; branding; exposure to the weather; forced calisthenics; forced consumption of any food, liquor, beverage, drug, or other substance; and subjection to extreme mental stress, including extended deprivation of sleep or rest or extended isolation.

Wisconsin forbids physical brutality (including whipping, beating, and branding); forced consumption of any food, liquor, beverage, drug, or other substances; forced confinement; and any other forced activity.

Kentucky joins these five states in specifically prohibiting the forced consumption of liquor or drug for purposes of initiation.

California, Florida, Kentucky, and Maine require state governing boards and agencies to establish standards, promulgate rules and regulations, and designate appropriate penalties to implement prohibitions against hazing. Where institutional lia-

Table 2.4
Who May be Held Liable for Hazing

State	Anyone Engaged in Hazing	Corporation, Association, Organ[1]	Administrator, Employee, Faculty Member, Person in Charge	Officer, Director, Governing Board Member	School or College	Reporting of Hazing Required
Alabama	X					X
Arkansas	X					X
California	X	X		X		
Florida	X					
Illinois	X					
Kentucky	X	X	X			
Louisiana	X					
Maine	X	X				
Maryland	X					
Massachusetts	X				X	
New Jersey	X					X
New York	X					
N. Carolina	X					
Ohio	X		X[2]	X	X[5]	
Oregon	X					
Rhode Island	X		X[3]			
Texas	X		X[4]	X[1]		X
Virginia	X					
Wisconsin	X					

[1] These seem specifically to target sororities and fraternities and their officers.
[2] Applies to persons who knew or reasonably should have known of the hazing and did not make a reasonable attempt to prevent it.
[3] Requires knowingly permitting hazing.
[4] Requires knowingly permitting, encouraging, aiding, or assisting in hazing or acquiescing in the commission of hazing.
[5] Mandatory liability if administrator, employee, or faculty member is held liable.

bility is not specifically provided by statute, the courts may impose it under the theory that the individual committing the hazing is an institutional official, an agent of the institution, acting on the institution's behalf. This would be another example of the use of the "deep pocket" theory since an institution is likely to have broader insurance coverage or greater resources than an individual.

Defenses. The Florida statute specifies that an individual's willingness to engage in "forced" activities doesn't negate the "forced" nature of the activities if *forced* means *required.* This means that an initiate eager to participate in the forced consumption of alcohol as part of initiation may still recover in tort for injury resulting from that forced consumption. This provision establishes a custodial relationship when someone is compelled to engage in activities that result in injury.

The Ohio statute specifies that the victim's negligence or consent or assumption of the risk is not a defense. This is similar in scope to the Florida statute, with the addition of the notion of assumption of the risk.

Assumption of the risk occurs when a person agrees in advance to relieve another of a duty of care toward the person and to proceed to take the chance of injury from a known risk resulting from what the other may do or leave undone. For example, an initiate is a premed major who knows that forced ingestion of large quantities of alcoholic beverages in a very short span of time will result in alcohol poisoning and may lead to unconsciousness and death. If the initiate agrees to proceed anyway, the initiate has assumed the risk of the known injury. Having proceeded with full knowledge and understanding of the consequences, the initiate has assumed the risk of that injury and relieved the fraternity of its duty not to expose the initiate to harm. The Ohio statute, however, establishes a custodial relationship for any initiation rite that causes injury, and allows the injured party to recover under circumstances that would preclude recovery in any other case.

The Ohio statute does allow as an affirmative defense for an institution that it had and was *actively* enforcing a policy against hazing at the time of the hazing. Whether this defense will be sufficient to shield the institution from liability will depend on the particular facts involved.

Caveat Lector

As stated at the beginning of this chapter, legislative enactments and court decisions between the time of writing and the time of

Table 2.5
Penalties[1] for Hazing

State	Fine[4]	Imprison-ment[5]	Both	Forfeit Public Funds	Forfeit Scholar-ships & Awards	Deprive of Inst. Sanctions/ Approval	Expul-sion
Alabama	X	X	X	X	X	X	
Arkansas	X	X	X				X
California	X	X	X	X	X	X	
Florida	X					X	X
Illinois	X	X	X				
Kentucky						X	X
Louisiana	X	X	X				
Maine						X	X
Maryland	X	X	X				
Mass.	X	X	X				
New Jersey	X	X	X				
New York	X	X					
N. Carolina	X	X	X				X[6]
Ohio	X	X					
Oregon	X						
Rhode Island[2]	X	X	X				
Texas	X	X	X				X[7]
Virginia[3]	X	X					X
Wisconsin	X	X	X				

[1] These states all provide criminal liability for hazing as a misdemeanor or infraction.

[2] Rhode Island considers tattooing or permanent disfigurement occurring as a result of hazing to be mayhem, punishable by imprisonment for a period of from one to ten years.

[3] Virginia considers hazing that causes an injury (such as mayhem or death) that would constitute a felony to be a felony.

[4] Range from $10 to $5,000.

[5] Range from ten days to one year.

[6] Failure to expel a student is a misdemeanor.

[7] Any teacher, instructor, faculty member, officer or director, or governing board member is to be discharged immediately from his/her position and is ineligible for reinstatement in state-supported institutions for three years.

publication may have affected what is written here. The reader is urged to confer with competent counsel before proceeding.

Conclusion

Institutions without policies governing possession and consumption of alcoholic beverages can no longer maintain a posture of benign neglect. Institutions with such policies can no longer be complacent or ambivalent about enforcing their policies. All institutions, especially those with sororities and fraternities, must be more intentional in confronting and addressing alcohol-related issues. Failure to be intentional is reasonably likely to create a serious risk of endangering the fiscal health and/or life of the institution.

References

Gulland, E. E., & Flournoy, A. C. (1985). *Universities, colleges, and alcohol: An overview of tort liability issues.* White Paper on Student Alcohol Abuse Prepared for the American Council on Education, Washington, DC.

RESTATEMENT OF TORTS 2d, American Law Institute, Minneapolis, Minnesota.

Table of Cases

Bell v. Alpha Tau Omega Fraternity, Eta Epsilon Chapter, 642 P. 2d 161 (Nevada 1982).

Bradshaw v. Rawlings, 612 F. 2d 135 (3d Cir. 1979), *cert. denied*, 446 U.S. 090 (1980).

Davies v. Butler, 602 P. 2d 605 (Nevada 1979), *reh'g. denied*, 1980.

Figuly v. Knoll, 449 A. 2d 564 (New Jersey 1982).

Linn v. Rand, 356 A. 2d 15 (New Jersey 1976).

Rappaport v. Nichols, 156 A. 2d 1 (New Jersey 1959).

Soronen v. Olde Milford Inn, Inc., 218 A. 2d 630 (New Jersey 1966).

Stein v. Beta Rho Alumni Association, Inc., 621 P. 2d 632 (Oregon 1980).

Wiener v. Gamma Phi Chapter of Alpha Tau Omega, 485 P.2d 18 (Oregon 1971).

Table of Statutes
ALABAMA CODE 6-5-71 (1975).
ALABAMA CODE 16-1-23 (Supp. 1986).
ALASKA STATUTES 04.21.020 (1986).
ARIZONA REVISED STATUTES ANNOTATED 4.311 (Supp. 1986).
ARKANSAS STATUTES ANNOTATED 80-5501 (Supp. 1985).
ARKANSAS STATUTES ANNOTATED 80-5502 (Supp. 1985).
ARKANSAS STATUTES ANNOTATED 80-5503 (Supp. 1985).
ARKANSAS STATUTES ANNOTATED 80-5505 (Supp. 1985).
CALIFORNIA BUSINESS & PROFESSION CODE 25602.1 (West Supp. 1987).
CALIFORNIA EDUCATION CODE 32050 (West Supp. 1987).
CALIFORNIA EDUCATION CODE 32051 (West Supp. 1987).
CALIFORNIA EDUCATION CODE 32052 (West Supp. 1987).
COLORADO REVISED STATUTES 13-21-103 (1973).
1986 CONNECTICUT LEGISLATIVE SERVICE 338 7 (West).
DISTRICT OF COLUMBIA CODE ANNOTATED 25-121 (Supp. 1986).
FLORIDA STATUTES ANNOTATED 240.262 (West Supp. 1986).
FLORIDA STATUTES ANNOTATED 768.125 (West Supp. 1986).
GEORGIA CODE ANNOTATED 105-1205 (1984).
IDAHO CODE 23-808 (Supp. 1986).
1986 ILLINOIS LEGISLATIVE SERVICE 1381 1 (West).
ILLINOIS ANNOTATED STATUTES ch. 144, 222 (Smith-Hurd 1986).
INDIANA CODE ANNOTATED 7.1-5-10-15.5 (Burns Supp. 1986).
1986 IOWA LEGISLATIVE SERVICE 2265 12 (West).
KENTUCKY REVISED STATUTES 164.375 (Supp. 1986).
LOUISIANA REVISED STATUTES ANNOTATED 17:1801 (West 1982).
LOUISIANA REVISED STATUTES ANNOTATED 26:683 (West 1975).
MAINE REVISED STATUTES ANNOTATED tit. 28, 1401-1419 (Supp. 1986).
MAINE REVISED STATUTES ANNOTATED tit. 20-A 10004 (Supp. 1986).

MARYLAND ANNOTATED CODE art. 27, 268H (Supp.1986).

MASSACHUSETTS GENERAL LAWS ANNOTATED, ch. 231 60F (Supp. 1986).

MASSACHUSETTS GENERAL LAWS ANNOTATED, ch. 231 805 (Supp. 1986).

MASSACHUSETTS GENERAL LAWS ANNOTATED, ch. 269 17-19 (Supp. 1986).

MICHIGAN COMPILED LAWS ANNOTATED 436.22 (West 1986).

MINNESOTA STATUTES ANNOTATED 340.A801 (West Supp. 1986).

MISSOURI ANNOTATED STATUTES 537.053 (Vernon Supp. 1986).

NEW JERSEY STATUTES ANNOTATED 2C:40-3 (West 1982).

NEW MEXICO STATUTES ANNOTATED 41-11-1 (1986).

NEW YORK GENERAL OBLIGATION LAW 11-101 (McKinney, 1978).

NEW YORK PENAL LAW 120.16 (McKinney Supp. 1987).

NEW YORK PENAL LAW 240.25 (McKinney 1980).

NORTH CAROLINA GENERAL STATUTES 14-35 (1986).

NORTH CAROLINA GENERAL STATUTES 14-36 (1986).

NORTH CAROLINA GENERAL STATUTES 14-38 (1986).

NORTH DAKOTA CENTURY CODE 5-01-06 (Supp. 1985).

OHIO REVISED CODE ANNOTATED 2307.44 (Page Supp. 1985).

OHIO REVISED CODE ANNOTATED 2903.31 (Page Supp. 1985).

OHIO REVISED CODE ANNOTATED 4399.01 (Page 1982).

OREGON REVISED STATUTES 30.950 (1985).

OREGON REVISED STATUTES 30.955 (1985).

OREGON REVISED STATUTES 30.960 (1985).

OREGON REVISED STATUTES 163.197 (1985).

PENNSYLVANIA STATUTES ANNOTATED tit. 47, 4-497 (Purdon 1969).

RHODE ISLAND GENERAL LAWS 3-14—3-14-15 (Supp. 1986).

RHODE ISLAND GENERAL LAWS 11-21-1 (Supp. 1986).

RHODE ISLAND GENERAL LAWS 11-21-2 (Supp. 1986).

RHODE ISLAND GENERAL LAWS 11-21-3 (1981).

TENNESSEE CODE ANNOTATED 57-10-102 (Supp. 1986).

TEXAS EDUCATION CODE ANNOTATED 4.19 (Vernon 1972 & 1986).
UTAH CODE ANNOTATED 32A-14-1 (1986).
VERMONT STATUTES ANNOTATED tit. 7, 501 (1972).
VIRGINIA CODE 18.2-56 (1982).
WISCONSIN STATUTES ANNOTATED 940.26 (West Supp. 1986).
WYOMING STATUTES 12-5-502 (1986).

Chapter 3

Campus Responses to Changes in the Drinking Age

Caryl K. Smith

The national trend to raise the drinking age has encouraged colleges and universities to adopt comprehensive alcohol policies. There are other sound and compelling reasons to stiffen the campus rules about alcohol possession, sale, and consumption. These reasons are found in the liability that the institutions are facing in the courts for the actions resulting from alcohol use of their students and the problems that result from that use.

Campuses of all types and sizes need to analyze and document their unique situations in order to develop suitable policies, plans, programs, and the resources to support them. Traditional ways of managing campus events, from fraternity parties, philanthropic ventures, and concessions at athletic events, to beverages dispensed in the college union and at social gatherings, will have to be evaluated and may have to be modified under the new drinking laws. The policies developed should stress the individual's responsibility for oneself and one's actions when drinking alcohol, whether on or off campus, and provide for enhanced alcohol education efforts.

This chapter will briefly review the state drinking laws and the key liability issues for campus administrators on campuses where alcohol is possessed, consumed, or sold. A review of guidelines for campus action plans precedes details of how one campus developed and is implementing an action plan. Some representative program ideas are shared, as is a look at the attitudes and behaviors of college students in response to the new drinking laws and the campus policies.

State Drinking Laws

Numerous states have raised the minimum drinking age and imposed mandatory penalties for those convicted of driving while under the influence of alcohol. Other states have been spurred to take these statutory actions by a new federal law (Pub.L.98-363, signed by President Reagan on July 17, 1984) that applies an incentive for the states to raise their drinking ages to 21 or face the loss of some federal highway funds. Eighteen states had raised the minimum drinking age to 21 since that legislation went into effect and prior to 1986. In 1985, the *Chronicle of Higher Education* (Ingalls) reported the following status of the drinking ages for all states (see Table 3.1), and, since that time, only Hawaii has passed legislation to raise the minimum drinking age to 21. This legislation is, however, restrictive in that, without further action by the Hawaii state legislature, the drinking age will revert to 18 on October 1, 1991. Idaho passed legislation in February, 1987, to raise the minimum drinking age to 21, but this legislation was vetoed by the governor.

Wide variations exist in the state laws concerning the exemptions for consumption of some kinds of wine and beer. In South Dakota, the attorney general has filed a lawsuit to challenge the constitutionality of the federal law. Nine other states have joined South Dakota in this lawsuit. Contingency plans are built into the new drinking age laws of a few other states so that their 21 restrictions are reversible if the South Dakota suit is successful (Ingalls, 1985).

Liability Concerns

In the climate created by the new drinking laws, colleges and universities increasingly are in danger of being sued for

Table 3.1
A Comprehensive Review of the
Legal Drinking Ages for Each of the Fifty States

MINIMUM LEGAL DRINKING AGE

Age 18:
Hawaii (1972)	Louisiana (1984)	Vermont (1971)

Age 19:
Idaho (1972)	Montana (1979)	Wisconsin (1983)
Iowa (1978)	West Virginia (1983)*	Wyoming (1973)
Minnesota (1976)		

Age 21:
Alabama (1985)	Kansas (1985)	North Carolina (1985)
Alaska (1983)	Kentucky (1938)	North Dakota (1936)
Arizona (1984)	Maine (1985)	Ohio (1982)**
Arkansas (1957)	Maryland (1982)	Oklahoma (1983)
California (1933)	Massachusetts (1985)	Oregon (1935)
Colorado (1945)**	Michigan (1978)	Pennsylvania (1935)
Connecticut (1985)	Mississippi (1985)***	Rhode Island (1984)
Delaware (1983)	Missouri (1945)	South Carolina (1985)
District of	Nebraska (1984)	South Dakota (1984)**
Columbia (1934)**	Nevada (1933)	Tennessee (1984)***
Florida (1985)	New Hampshire (1985)	Texas (1985)
Georgia (1985)	New Jersey (1982)	Utah (1935)
Illinois (1980)	New Mexico (1934)	Virginia (1985)
Indiana (1934)	New York (1985)	Washington (1934)

Note: Date in parentheses indicates when age legislation was enacted.

Effective dates vary.
* Twenty-one for nonresidents.
** Indicates lower age for some kinds of wine and beer consumption.
*** Indicates lower age for minors accompanied by their parents or for military personnel.

property damage or injuries resulting from students' drinking. It is likely that the campuses will lose more of these lawsuits than they would have previously. The colleges must abide by the drinking laws and educate the campus community about these laws and the dangers of alcohol use, while neither going beyond tolerable bounds of control nor violating the rights of individual privacy. The time when student affairs professionals could be casual about their knowledge of drinking laws is past.

The American Council on Education, in a white paper by Gulland and Flournay (1985), emphasizes four college functions that can be sources of liability and that demand due consideration from all student affairs practitioners. These functions are the college's limited role as supervisor of student conduct, as property owner, as seller of alcohol, and as "social host."

Each institution's policy ought to reflect the campus traditions in dealing with the alcohol issue, as well as the requirements of law and the expectation that students have personal responsibility for their conduct. Colleges and universities should develop programs to educate the students about the laws, the policies, and the dangers of alcohol abuse. Institutions can best demonstrate compliance with the "duty to care" when the rules governing student drinking are realistic and are consistently enforced.

Guidelines for Campuses

As campuses examine their circumstances and develop or revise policies relating to alcohol, the issues and concerns are many. An Inter-Association Task Force on Alcohol Issues developed model guidelines for a reasonable campus policy that permits the possession, consumption, or service of alcohol (See appendix to Chapter 6 for the complete text of this document). Each of the following topics is addressed:

1. Legal Requirements. A summary of the state laws concerning the drinking age, the regulations for the sale of alcohol, and the possession of open containers and of other laws pertinent to the specific jurisdiction.
2. University Requirements. A comprehensive alcohol policy to address (a) locations where alcoholic beverages are permitted to be possessed, served, and consumed by

persons of legal drinking age; (b) locations where alcoholic beverages are permitted to be sold; (c) guidelines for public and private social events that involve alcoholic beverages within the institution's jurisdiction; (d) an explicit statement concerning the use or nonuse of alcoholic beverages at membership recruitment functions; (e) a specific statement concerning the use or nonuse of alcoholic beverages in athletic facilities or at athletic events that should apply equally to all constituencies; (f) guidelines for any marketing, advertising, and promotion of alcoholic beverages on campus or at campus events involving alcohol; and (g) procedures for adjudicating violations of the alcohol policy.

The task force also developed guidelines for the beer and liquor industries to follow in campus advertising and promotions. Campus administrators should be familiar with the details of these recommendations.

Diary of a Campus Action Plan

The University of Kansas, like other campuses in states where the drinking laws are changing, has been working to meet both its responsibilities to the laws and to the educational mission of the institution. Kansas, historically a dry state, remains so today with the exception that persons 21 or older are able to purchase liquor by the drink in private clubs. Until action of the Kansas Legislature in April 1985, persons 18 or older could purchase cereal malt beverages (3.2% beer). Following national trends and federal legislation, the Kansas Legislature changed the state laws so that the legal drinking age for cereal malt beverages was raised to 19 years on July 1, 1985, and to 21 in 1987. In November 1986, Kansas voters approved an amendment to the state constitution to allow the sale of liquor-by-the-drink; this could take effect by late 1987.

The University of Kansas, a doctoral-degree-granting university, has approximately 24,000 students on the main campus in Lawrence. About 16,000 of these are undergraduates.

Nearly 6,500 students live on campus in residence halls, scholarship halls, or university apartments.

The University of Kansas experience of how one institution has dealt with changes in the state drinking age is presented as a diary in an attempt to assist other schools engaged in a similar process. It is not a comprehensive answer, only a report of the responses on one campus.

April 1985. The Vice Chancellor for Student Affairs at the University of Kansas appointed a special task force to consider the implications of the new Kansas drinking laws and to recommend where new or revised policies or procedures would be needed and what their content should be. The task force was chaired by the director of the Kansas Unions, who is the person holding the license to sell cereal malt beverages on the campus. Other task force members were representatives from the fraternities, the residence hall system, the university police, the student newspaper, the office of the university general counsel, the student health center, the student assistance center, and public relations. The membership of the task force included students, faculty, administrative staff, and alumni. The scope of the task force was to consider the effect of the new Kansas drinking laws on the campus, including

1. the consumption of cereal malt beverages (3.2% beer) on campus and at university-sanctioned events,
2. the marketing and sale of cereal malt beverages on campus,
3. the use of cereal malt beverages in university-owned housing units,
4. the enforcement of state and university regulations regarding alcoholic beverages and cereal malt beverages,
5. the concern for third-party liability as it could affect the university and registered student organizations,
6. the alcohol-abuse education programs available on campus, and
7. the plan for implementation of the recommendations of the task force.

April and May 1985. The task force met frequently, and

members prepared impact statements on selected areas of the university that would be affected by the law and policy changes. Each topical statement report dealt with specific aspects of the university and identified whether the effect concerned consumption, possession, sale, third-party liability, educational programming, or enforcement of the regulations. Each impact statement made recommendations for the university policies and procedures that would need to be modified or developed. The task force carefully reviewed each of the impact reports and the resulting recommendations.

June 1985. The task force report was completed, submitted, and accepted in its entirety by the Vice Chancellor and the Chancellor.

June-August 1985. Across the campus, follow up to the task force progressed toward the goal of implementing the recommendations of the task force by the beginning of fall semester. Specific tasks targeted for completion by the start of school were as follows: (a) development and approval of a University Alcohol and Cereal Malt Beverage Policy; (b) development of a brochure to be distributed in large numbers stating the university policy, relevant state statutes and their penalties, campus and local resources, and the importance of student awareness and responsibilities in alcohol use; (c) a summer mailing to all registered student organization leaders to apprise them of the changes effective in the fall; (d) a separate summer mailing to the leadership of each of the fraternities and sororities at the university (all fraternities/sororities are located in off-campus properties at the University of Kansas); (e) a complete review and updating of alcohol education programs and their materials; (f) plans to implement the new policies as they would affect the thousands of students living in on-campus housing units and to work closely with the student leadership of those housing units to develop new patterns for organized social events that previously were tied to the availability of cereal malt beverages; and (g) plans to provide opportunities for campus-wide student leaders to participate in informational sessions about the new policies and laws shortly after their return to the campus.

Other areas of the campus began work to bring their operations into line with the revised university policies. The staff of the student newspaper revised their advertising policies and provided appropriate training for their sales representatives, and the athletic department developed effective means to notify event patrons of the new, more restrictive policies.

August 1985. The return of the students to campus brought opportunities for consultation and detailed planning as orientation week events were transformed from their traditional formats into activities in compliance with the new drinking age laws and policies. Informational meetings were held with student leaders from the fraternities and sororities, alumni advisors, and house corporation board presidents of each of these groups. In the K.U. situation, with these housing units all located off campus and privately owned by the corporations, the university had the responsibility to inform those in key corporate leadership roles. In many cases, the national organizations have issued policies pertaining to chapter activities and the use of alcohol.

The Executive Director of Alcohol Beverage Control for Kansas appeared at an open meeting to which student leaders in key campus organizations were invited. The director of the university police department and a representative of the office of the university general counsel were present. All three presented their views and concerns about the changes and the resulting impact on the campus; they also answered questions from the student leaders. The student leaders expressed concern about their abilities to influence and control their members in a variety of circumstances, about their own liability for events that involve alcohol, and about making a transition from a campus situation in which alcohol has been an integral part of the social scene. The meeting was informative and supportive for the student leaders. It also revealed to the administrators present that these students needed sound advice and quality educational materials in coping with the issues.

Fall Semester 1985. Student leaders reported few problems with acceptance of the new laws and policies. One editorial did appear in the student newspaper protesting the strong stand taken by the university, especially in the on-campus housing units, but the staff in those housing units reported few problems and generally good cooperation by the residents. The social events that had previously dispensed large amounts of cereal malt beverages were reorganized with different enticements, and in several cases established new attendance records. Alcohol Awareness Week events were well attended and accepted. (An ongoing concern is how well the events held in athletic department facilities are complying with the new laws and policies, and work continues on this topic.)

September 1986. A follow-up study to the Special Task Force Report on the New Drinking Laws was completed and submitted to the Vice Chancellor. In addition to progress reports on the original recommendations (33 were completed, 5 were in process, and 5 were not completed), new recommendations were made suggesting modifications in (a) the university alcohol policy (to make it consistent with the new Board of Regents policy); (b) the student newspaper's advertising policy (to make it consistent with newly revised state statutes); and (c) the enforcement patterns of alcohol-related policies at events where large numbers of off-campus nonstudents were present. Work to implement the new recommendations began.

November 1986. In response to a request of all Kansas state schools by the Board of Regents, the Vice Chancellor appointed an Alcohol and Substance Abuse Task Force to further evaluate information available to the campus community about the illegal use of controlled substances and alcohol; to continue evaluation of the effectiveness of existing drug and alcohol education programs; and to recommend additional educational programs or activities to combat drug and alcohol abuse on campus, if needed.

February 1987. A campus student leader organized and held a campus-wide discussion on alcohol issues for the leaders of student organizations; this was held as a follow up to the open meeting held in August 1985. Invited guests and resource people were from the same campus organizations and offices and state agencies as at the open meeting. Emphasis was on the practical aspects of managing campus student activities within the current (new) drinking laws.

Impact on Small Colleges

A recent survey of several NASPA regional representatives, located on small college campuses, found similar approaches and results. One conclusion, in any size institution, seems to be that alcohol cannot be successfully controlled on campus unless certain positive steps are taken. Some successful approaches include training peer advisors (good role models *do* make a difference); channeling institutional funds into alcohol-related education and programming; and educating residence hall staff about the new laws and providing training for them in intervention techniques for problem situations.

Many small educational institutions in Massachusetts are undergoing dramatic changes for two reasons: insurance companies in the state refuse to insure any alcohol vendor and the Governor of Massachusetts has made drunk driving a major issue. New England, as a whole, seems to be adopting a severe approach to alcohol abuse or misuse. It is not uncommon to be stopped on the roadways for random alcohol breath tests. Persons under the age of 21 are not allowed into clubs or bars, and those caught with false identification face severe sanctions.

Most students on small college campuses support the new laws but have not completely changed their drinking habits. Several small institutions have established policies for "seniors only" residence halls where alcohol is permitted for private consumption. Historically, most small private colleges in the Midwest have not allowed alcohol on campus, so the new laws have little impact on these institutions.

Other Campuses

Other campuses have used similar approaches to comply with the changing laws. Kansas State University appointed an Ad Hoc Committee on Campus Drinking Policies, which reported to the campus in August 1985 and recommended a comprehensive policy statement that was adopted by the President. Rutgers University had an early start on campus alcohol policy concerns. The Rutgers University Committee on the Use of Alcohol reported to the University in May 1981, a timely report since the New Jersey Legislature raised the drinking age to 21 in 1982. The Rutgers report recommended development of alcohol education and training programs and stressed the need for a central university authority to oversee implementation of the recommendations.

Another model for sharing information and programs is the New England College Alcohol Network, composed of over 250 health educators, deans, and counselors from almost 100 colleges and universities. Formed in 1982, the group still operates informally to coordinate and share ideas and efforts and to reduce the isolation that persons working with college alcohol problems have often felt. The isolation, created by expectations that one person or one office will take care of it for the campus, may be eased as more institutions are becoming active in response to societal needs and legislative actions. Some campuses have done surveys to determine what other institutions are doing to manage the legal age and alcohol-usage issues. Both the University of Dayton and Iowa State University developed surveys to inquire about on-campus alcohol use, especially concerning use in the residence halls.

Campus Educational Programs

Educational programming and the creative use of available resources are challenges for student affairs practitioners faced with changing drinking-age laws. Kansas State University received a grant from the state that assisted the university in addressing campus issues resulting from changes in the state drinking-age laws. The project provided print-ready materials to assist in the dissemination of information. A conference was held in the summer of 1985 to share the resources, program ideas, and graphic materials with personnel from all aspects of higher education in Kansas.

Strategies to impact the campus environment as a means to reduce campus and student alcohol problems were developed by Bryan (1984). These strategies include a campus referral system to disseminate information and to utilize trained peers as well as faculty and staff; comprehensive campus information systems to assist students in coping with reality and their emotions; an all-campus alcohol awareness task force; and a university-wide commitment to working with drinking concerns. Colleges and universities developing their own strategies, projects, or programs should be aware of the research grant awards made by BACCHUS. Awards have been made for projects designed to assess the impact of alcohol education programs. Preference in selection was given to projects that can serve as models to other colleges or universities. Some representative campus programs and services in support of alcohol education are briefly mentioned below:

1. An alcohol "myth of the week" is published in the student newspaper (Kansas).
2. Public service announcements on alcohol awareness topics are aired on local radio stations (Kansas).
3. A Guide to Responsible Hosting is a regular part of residence hall staff and student leadership training programs (Kansas).
4. A Directory of Alcohol and Drug Education and Treatment Resources in the Community and at the University is distributed widely (Kansas).
5. A Dry Bar, an on-campus night spot, features snacks and nonalcoholic beverages, as well as student entertainment (Ohio State University and University of Louisville).
6. A Nonalcoholic Beverages (NABs) bar is set up on campus and serves drinks to students, staff, and faculty passing by (Kansas).
7. "Mocktail" parties are held with staff serving nonalcoholic beverages to convince students that they can party without alcohol (University of Maryland-College Park).
8. A wrecked car is positioned against a tree on the central part of campus during Alcohol Awareness Week as a grim and eye-catching reminder (Kansas).
9. An alcohol awareness ideas contest in which the grand prize is 100 gallons of milk is held (Kansas).
10. Academic departments sponsor a Friday or Saturday night at the on-campus "dry" pub, with faculty serving and giving alcohol awareness information to guests (University of Louisville).

Fraternities on a number of campuses have taken dramatic steps to restrict or eliminate alcohol as a part of regular operations. Most dramatic is the national movement to "dry rush" programs. Among the 150 campuses that reportedly adopted dry rush for 1985-1986 are University of Georgia, Florida State University, Ball State University, University of Tulsa, University of Oklahoma, Oklahoma State University, Syracuse University, University of Alabama, and Auburn University. A majority of campuses with dry rush programs reported increases in numbers of fraternity pledges. Chapters reported that while they were developing creative methods to lure interested rushees, they felt that they were getting to know the new students better than previously.

Alpha Tau Omega National Fraternity has imposed several restrictions on the ATO chapters across the country: dry rush, invitation-only social events, a ban on selling alcohol, a trained bartender to serve drinks, nonalcoholic beverages served at the bar, and a ban on sponsoring or cosponsoring any function with a beverage distributor or brewing company. ATO took these actions after being unable to obtain insurance for its chapters (Staff, *National On Campus Report*, 1986).

College Student Responses to the Changes

It is still early to have concrete data on the results of the changes in the drinking-age laws on college students. One liberal arts college with traditional-age students administered a comprehensive questionnaire that revealed some rather dramatic contradictions in student attitudes (Perkins & Berkowitz, 1985). The students supported the law in theory as important for others, but personally ignored the law in their own drinking practice. The students apparently did not believe that they were likely to do harm to themselves or others.

Students say drinking may drop temporarily, but that ways to get around the new drinking-age laws will be found and used. False identification cards, drinking in cars and off campus, trying to convince older friends to provide alcoholic beverages, and increasing use of drugs are approaches predicted or reported from a variety of campuses.

The United States Student Association and several state student organizations have criticized Congress for developing and passing the federal legislation. Student organizations feel that the drinking-age laws are discriminatory to the 18-21 age population. Some campus organizations have complained about the specific policies being enforced and have made counter proposals. At least one campus student government is conducting extensive polls to garner support for a more moderate approach than that taken by that particular private university. One publication reporting national campus events offered the opinion that the 21 drinking-age laws violate the Fourteenth and Twenty-first Amendments and are not the answer to alcohol abuse problems (Staff, *National On Campus Report*, 1985).

Conclusion

Continuous concerns about alcohol use and abuse by students in America's colleges and universities have been the basis for extensive education programs and projects. Recent federal legislation mandating that the states raise their legal drinking ages to 21 by not later than 1987 has provided additional incentives to leadership in higher education to review and implement institutional policies and programs that will comply. In addition, compelling reasons for stiffening regulations concerning student drinking are found in court actions that hold third parties liable for alcohol-related damages. College and university student affairs administrators must play a key role in responding to the numerous changes that these laws bring to the institutions and to their students. They have the opportunity and obligation to assume leadership in responding to both the educational mission and the legal requirements of the drinking-age laws and the needs for alcohol use and abuse programs. Student affairs professionals should focus their efforts on campus programs and plans that would assist student leaders in dealing with increased needs for creative social programming and events consistent with the stipulations of the new drinking laws and the accompanying modifications in campus policies.

References

Bryan,W. A.(1984). Environmental strategies to reduce student drinking problems. In D. A. Boulton, W. A. Bryan, J. F. Corey, J. E. Marshall, D. D. McIntire, T.H. Stafford, (Eds.). *Student Services, Third Compendium of Papers by Student Services Officers of the University of North Carolina*, pp. 67-76. Chapel Hill, NC: University of North Carolina.

Gulland, E., & Flournay, A. (1985, October). *Universities, colleges, and alcohol: An overview of tort liability issues*. White Paper on Student Alcohol Abuse prepared for the American Council on Education, Washington, DC.

Ingalls, Z. (1985, October 30). Higher drinking age won't solve problems of alcohol abuse by students, officials say. *The Chronicle of Higher Education*, pp. 23-24.

Perkins, H., & Berkowitz, A. (1985, October). *College students' attitudinal and behavioral responses to a drinking-age law change: Stability and contradiction in the campus setting*. Paper presented at the annual meeting of the New York State Sociological Association, Rochester, NY.

Staff. (1985, March/April). Alcohol policy recommended. *NASPA Forum*, 5(6), pp. 1, 11.

Staff. (1986, January 6). Campus Capsules. *National On-Campus Report. 14*(1), p. 5.

Chapter 4

College Students' Drinking Patterns and Problems

Ruth C. Engs and David J. Hanson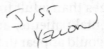

Many studies over the past 30 years have examined college students' drinking patterns. On the whole, male college students drink more than female college students. Drinking by students is not unique to the United States; in fact, a higher incidence of drinking among male university students has been reported in Australia, Canada, Colombia, England, India, and Ireland. Studies over the past decade have also indicated that white college students drink more frequently and in higher quantities than black college students. These drinking patterns have possible significance for education, prevention, and intervention strategies by student affairs personnel.

The Gender Differential

Within the past ten years, more than 30 published papers have reported more frequent and higher consumption of alcoholic beverages among males as compared to females. The only exception has been Reiskin and Wechsler's (1981) survey of students who used the services of a campus mental health center.

However, data from students at the same university who did not use the center are consistent with the other studies.

Several reasons have been suggested for the differential in drinking patterns between men and women. Windham and Aldridge (1965) referred to the traditional belief that the use and abuse of alcohol was primarily a male custom. Clark (1967) suggested that drinking differences are based largely upon the expectation that female sex roles are characterized by what he termed "conventionality." By this he referred to the "acceptance of the dominant 'official' standards of morality and propriety" (p. 2). Drinking is often a symbol that differentiates the sexes, and women tend to be economically dependent on and subordinate to men. In this regard, Knupfer, Fink, and Goffman (1963) emphasized that "other members of the population who do not earn their living by paid work also have more restricted drinking privileges than adult free males—for example, children, prisoners, mental patients, and persons on relief" (p. 14).

It would appear that the double standard in alcohol use may indeed be decreasing. Wechsler and McFadden (1976) referred to sex differences in adolescent alcohol use as "a disappearing phenomenon." While Blane and Hewitt's (1977) analysis of the literature led them to conclude that it was uncertain whether sex differences in drinking patterns had changed much between 1965 and 1975, other research supports the "disappearing phenomenon" thesis. For example, Straus and Bacon's (1953) college study found a 16 percentage point differential between the sexes whereas Hanson's comparable 1972 study at 37 colleges and universities found this reduced to only five percentage points (Hanson, 1974). Shortly thereafter, Glassco (1975) found only three percentage points between males and females in his study of college seniors. Later, Hanson (1977) found an equal percentage of males and females to be drinkers at 17 of his earlier-sampled institutions. Although some studies have reported a difference (Engs, 1977; Engs & Hanson, 1986), the apparently general reduction of the differential between males and females in the incidence of drinking is consistent with the reduction of the double standard in sexual behavior, smoking behavior, voting, and other behaviors.

Wilsnack and Wilsnack (1978) point out that increased

drinking among females might be a result of the women's move- ment and changes in women's roles, especially changes that in- volve exposure to formerly masculine environments and roles. They suggest that changes in sex roles might (a) increase wom- en's exposure to alcohol and opportunities to drink; (b) modify traditional norms against female drinking, thereby making drinking more permissible; and (c) offer females new goals and aspirations, thus causing stress that alcohol might be used to reduce.

Berkowitz and Perkins (1985) conducted a five-year longitu- dinal study of drinking at a small college in New York for the period 1979-1984. Although there was a significant narrowing of the gender gap in the frequency and the volume of alcohol con- sumed, they found that males continued to experience more problems due to drinking and differed in alcohol attitudes as well as in their motivations for drinking.

Beverage Preferences

Straus and Bacon (1953) found that for males who drank, 72% most often consumed beer, 21% consumed spirits, and 7% con- sumed wine. For females, the favored beverages were spirits (43%), beer (41%), and wine (16%). About 25 years later, Engs (1977) found that beer remained the most popular among men and spirits remained the most popular among women. Among the men, 81% drank beer at least once a year, 75% drank spirits, and 65% drank wine. Among the women, 74% drank spirits at least once a year, 65% drank wine, and 61% drank beer.

In their sample of New England college students, Wechsler and McFadden (1979) and Wechsler and Rohman (1981) found that the beverage preferences for males were as follows: beer (95%), spirits (92%), and wine (86%). Among females, the high- est proportion drank spirits (95%), while 91% consumed wine and 77%, beer. Beer was preferred by both males and females at a large Midwestern university (Strange & Schmidt, 1979). At a small private college in western New York, Banks and Smith (1980) found that males were more likely to prefer beer while female choices were more evenly distributed among beer, wine, and spirits. In a private college in Boston, Biber, Hashway, and

Annick (1980) found that males preferred beer while the first choice of females was liquor, followed by wine as a second choice.

In a sample of students at colleges across the United States, Engs and Hanson (1985) found beer to be preferred by males, wine to be preferred by females, and distilled spirits to be equally preferred by males and females. Similarly, in two samples of students at an urban university, Reiskin and Wechsler (1981) found that men reported significantly more frequent consumption of beer than did women. However, there were no significant differences between the sexes, in either sample, in the consumption frequency of either wine or spirits.

Males at the University of Maryland reported higher frequencies of both beer and whiskey consumption than did females, while women reported drinking dinner wine more often than men (Johnson & Selacek, 1979). Likewise, among students at Indiana University, males preferred beer while females preferred wine (Wakefield, 1982).

At a state university in the Southeast, Trotter (1982) found that the alcoholic beverages most often drunk by males were beer (75%), liquor (21%), and wine (4%), while those most often drunk by females were liquor (64%), wine (20%), and beer (16%). Among students at a large Midwestern university, men were likely to drink beer and straight liquor, while women were more likely to drink wine and mixed drinks (Keane & Swinford, 1984).

Drinking Locations

At a university in Maryland, males reported drinking most frequently at what the researchers (Johnson & Sedlacek, 1979) called public places (e.g., car, ballgame, concert), while females drank most often in restaurants or lounges. Among students at a university in Texas, men were more likely to drink in their own home, a friend's home, or a dormitory, while women were more likely to drink in a restaurant, nightclub, or bar (Trotter, 1982).

Drinking is greatly influenced by the social context in which it occurs. In this regard, Waller and Lorch (1977) reported that male alcohol consumption tends to occur in drinking groups of the same sex, while female drinking most often occurs in mixed groups. This finding is also supported by Wechsler & Rohman (1981).

Biber et al. (1980) found that among students at a large private college in Boston, both males and females preferred to drink in large group settings. However, compared to males, females preferred drinking in structured social situations (nightclubs, bars, taverns, restaurants, or at home with parents) to drinking in social environments (dormitories, athletic events, concerts, campus grounds, or parks) or in intimate surroundings (with one person or alone).

Biber et al. (1980) observed that drinking is incorporated into a wider range of activities for men than for women. Men are much more likely to drink outdoors, at athletic events, alone, in small groups of other men, or in small groups of men and women. Such contexts are typically associated with heavy drinking. But women in mixed group situations tend to conform to sex-role stereotypes regarding appropriate drinking behavior. Thus, drinking in such situations tends to limit the consumption of alcohol by women.

Drinking Problems by Gender

Male college students tend to have a higher percentage of drinking problems compared to female students. In response to the query "Does drinking interfere with school? (i.e., missing class)," 15.1% of the male drinkers at a Western university agreed that it sometimes did, while 7.9% of the female drinkers responded in the same way (Kuder & Madson, 1976). When asked "Do you stop drinking before you get drunk?," 29.1% of the female drinkers reported that they always did, while only 19.4% of the males responded in the same way.

In comparison to females, males at a Maryland university reported that they had been drunk more often and had driven a car more often after consuming at least three drinks (Johnson & Sedlacek, 1979). However, Cox and Baker (1982) found that males and females had comparable distributions of problem drinking scores on the Michigan Alcoholism Screening Test.

At a Midwestern university, males reported significantly

more alcohol-related problems with family, relatives, friends, neighbors, school or employer, the law, finances, and health or injury (Kozicki, 1982). In their study at a public university in Illinois, Peterson and Allen (1983) found that males reported significantly more drinking-related mishaps (accidents, damage to property, etc.) than did females. Males also reported more problem-related reasons for drinking.

Reiskin and Wechsler (1981) reported that in a sample of students at an urban university in New England, 71% of the men and 54% of the women reported being intoxicated at least once in the previous year. Being intoxicated was defined as "when alcohol causes you to lose control of physical activities, or to get unsteady, aggressive, or sick to your stomach" (p. 720).

Data collected by Wechsler and Rohman (1981) at 34 New England colleges revealed that males reported a substantially higher rate of problems arising from their drinking, a finding also reported by Walfish, Wentz, Benzing, Brennan, and Champ (1981) at a large university in Florida.

A recent study at a Michigan university (Rappaport, Cooper, & Leemaster, 1984) revealed that more males reported damaging property, preparing less for exams, attending class less frequently, and experiencing blackouts. More males also reported drinking with the specific intent of becoming drunk, drinking while driving, driving while drunk, drinking before class, and drinking alone.

At a small private college in upstate New York (Berkowitz & Perkins, 1985), three general categories of problems due to drinking were examined: (a) physical injuries to self or others, property damage, or fighting; (b) damaged social relations (e.g., behavior that resulted in negative reactions from others, or damaged friendships or relationships); and (c) impaired academic performance (e.g., inefficiency in homework, classroom, or lab performance; late papers, missed classes or exams; or failure to study for exams). Significantly more males reported the first two categories, and while more also reported impaired academic performance, the difference was not statistically significant. Engs & Hanson (1986) also found that male students have more drinking problems.

Table 4.1
Problems Due to Drinking Among Those Who Drink Once a Year or More by Sex and Race in Percent

Problem	SEX		RACE	
	Men	Women	White	Black
Hangover	78.2	69.4+	74.8	46.2+
Vomited	51.7	43.8+	48.2	26.3+
Drove car after drinking	67.7	46.2+	56.0+	31.6+
Drove car after knowing had too much to drink	48.9	29.9+	38.7+	14.0+
Drank while driving	54.0	30.5+	40.7+	24.0+
Came to class after drinking	13.0	6.0+	8.7	7.0
Cut class because of drinking	14.7	7.7+	10.6	8.2
Missed class because of drinking	31.1	23.7+	27.7+	10.5+
Stopped for DWI	1.7	.9+	1.1	0.0
Criticized for drinking too much	13.9	8.8+	10.8	8.8
Had trouble with the law	7.1	1.9+	4.0	1.2
Lost job	.2	.4	6.0	4.7
Received lower grade	7.8	4.8+	1.8	.6
Problems with school administration	3.0	1.0+	12.1	10.5
Got into fight	18.1	8.2+	8.1	5.3
Thought have drinking problem	11.0	6.3+	.2	.6
Damaged property	18.3	4.1+	9.7	4.7

Note: Based upon data presented by Engs and Hanson (1986) as well as unpublished data.

Drinking Patterns and Problems by Race

A higher incidence of drinking frequency and quantity among white compared to black collegians has been reported by five studies extending back over 20 years. In their sample of New England college students, Wechsler and McFadden (1979) found an equal proportion of white males and females to be drinkers (96.7%) but a higher proportion of black males (98.5%) and a much lower proportion of black females to be drinkers (87.7%).

Engs (1977) found 22% of the white males in her sample to be heavy drinkers but only 5% of the black males to be heavy consumers. The proportion of such drinkers among female students of either race was about 5%. Wechsler and McFadden (1979) similarly found 30.0% of white but only 16.2% of black males to be frequent heavy drinkers. Of white females, 11.3% were frequent heavy drinkers, but only 3.7% of black women were. Kaplan (1979) also found heavy drinking to be more common among white male collegians, and Humphrey, Stephens, and Allen (1984) found that whites were more likely to drink to intoxication than were blacks. Engs and Hanson (1985) discovered that, of the students who drank, 26.4% of whites were heavy drinkers while only 7.3% of black students fell into that category.

Since white students tend to be more frequent and heavier drinkers, it is not surprising that they also appear to experience more problems due to drinking. Thus, Engs and Hanson (1986) found that a higher proportion of whites reported having experienced possible negative consequences of drinking (see Table 4.1).

Conclusion

It must be kept in mind that this paper includes reports that were based upon both individual universities and national samples of university students. Because of this mixture, generalizability might be difficult. However, most of the reports showed that a higher percentage of college men are likely to drink, to drink more often, to consume more, and to experience more drinking problems than women. While the gender differentials in drinking patterns and problems might be narrowing, males still have the major problems.

Similarly, a higher percentage of white collegians are likely to drink, to drink more often, to consume more, and to experience more drinking problems than black collegians. It appears that those at greatest risk of experiencing problems due to drinking are white males while those at least risk are black females (Hanson & Engs, 1986).

To be most effective, collegiate alcohol policies and programs must recognize and reflect the differential drinking patterns and problems of college students and aim programming at those groups exhibiting the most problem behaviors (Hanson & Engs, in press).

References

Banks, E., & Smith, M.R. (1980). Attitudes and background factors related to alcohol use among college students. *Psychological Reports, 46*, pp. 571-577.

Berkowitz, A.D., & Perkins, H.W. (1985). *Gender differences in collegiate drinking: Longitudinal trends and developmental patterns.* Paper presented at the American College Personnel Association Conference.

Biber, S.H., Hashway, R.N., & Annick, J.F. (1980). Drinking patterns of male and female collegians: Are the patterns converging? *Journal of College Student Personnel, 21*(4), pp. 349-353.

Blane, H.T., & Hewitt, L.E. (1977). *Alcohol and youth; an analysis of the literature, 1960-75.* U.S. National Institute on Alcohol Abuse and Alcoholism.

Clark, W. (1967). *Sex roles and alcoholic beverage use.* (Working Paper Number 16). Berkeley, CA: Mental Research Institute, Drinking Practices Study.

Cox, W.M., & Baker, E.K. (1982). Sex differences in locus of control and problem drinking among college students. *Bulletin of the Society of Psychologists in Substance Abuse, 1*(3), pp. 104-106.

Engs, R.C. (1977). Drinking patterns and drinking problems of college students. *Journal of Studies on Alcohol, 38*, pp. 2144-2156.

Engs, R.C., & Hanson, D.J. (1985). The drinking patterns and problems of college students. *Journal of Alcohol and Drug Education, 31*(1), pp. 65-83.

Engs, R.C. & Hanson, D.J. (1986, August). *Correlates of drinking problems and knowledge of drinking among collegians over time: Implications for education.* Paper presented at the National

Institute on Drug Abuse/National Institute on Alcoholism and Alcohol Abuse First National Conference on Alcohol and Drug Abuse Prevention, Washington, DC.

Glassco, K. (1975). Drinking habits of seniors in a southern university. *Journal of Alcohol and Drug Education, 21,* 25-29.

Hanson, D.J. (1974). Drinking attitudes and behaviors among college students. *Journal of Alcohol and Drug Education, 19,* pp. 6-14.

Hanson, D.J. (1977). Trends in drinking attitudes and behaviors among college students. *Journal of Alcohol and Drug Education, 22,* pp. 17-22.

Hanson, D.J., & Engs, R.C. (1986). Correlates of drinking problems among collegians. *The College Student Journal, 20,* pp. 141-146.

Hanson, D.J., & Engs, R.C. (in press). Black college students' drinking patterns. In B. Forster & J. Salloway (Eds.), *Chemical Bonds: The Socio-Cultural Matrix of Alcohol and Drug Use.* Monterey, CA: Wadsworth.

Humphrey, J., Stephens, V., & Allen, D. (1983). Race, sex, marijuana use and alcohol intoxication in college students. *Journal of Studies on Alcohol, 44*(4), pp. 733-738.

Johnson, D.H., & Sedlacek, W.E. (1979). *Drinking attitudes and behaviors of incoming freshmen.* University of Maryland.

Kaplan, M.S. (1979). Patterns of alcoholic beverage use among college students. *Journal of Alcohol and Drug Education, 24,* pp. 26-40.

Keane, J.S., & Swinford, P.L. (1984). *Alcohol use among students at a large Midwestern university.* Paper presented at the annual meeting of the American Psychological Association, Toronto, Ontario, Canada.

Knupfer, G.R., Fink, W.C., & Goffman, A.G. (1963). *California drinking practices study No.6: Related to amount of drinking in an urban community.* Berkeley, CA: State of California Department of Public Health.

Kozicki, Z.A. (1982). The measurement of drinking problems among students at a Midwestern university. *Journal of Alcohol and Drug Education, 27*(3), pp. 61-72.

Kuder, J.M., & Madson, D.L. (1976). College student use of alcoholic beverages. *Journal of College Student Personnel, 17,* pp. 142-144.

Peterson, J.S., & Allen, H.A. (1983). Internal-external control and motivations for alcohol use among college students. *Psychological Reports, 52(3),* pp. 692-694.

Rappaport, R.J., Cooper, A., & Leemaster, H. (1984). *Student alcohol misuse: The negative effects of drinking in college.* Central Michigan University Counseling Center.

Reiskin, H., & Wechsler, H. (1981). Drinking among college students using a campus mental health center. *Journal of Studies on Alcohol, 42,* pp. 716-724.

Strange, C.C., & Schmidt, M.R. (1979). College student perceptions of alcohol use and differential drinking behavior. *Journal of College Student Personnel, 20(1),* pp. 73-79.

Straus, R., & Bacon, S.D. (1953). *Drinking in college.* New Haven: Yale University Press.

Trotter, R.T. (1982). Ethnic and sexual patterns of alcohol use. Anglo and Mexican American college students. *Adolescence, 17(66),* pp. 305-325.

Wakefield, L.M. (1982). *Alcohol and other drug use among undergraduates at Indiana University, Bloomington, including a comparison between I.U. students and the state's high school population.* Indiana University Bureau of Educative Studies & Testing. (ERIC Document Reproduction Service No. ED 226 680).

Walfish, S., Wentz, D., Benzing, P., Brennan, F., & Champ, S. (1981). Alcohol abuse on a college campus: A needs assessment. *Evaluation and Program Planning, 4,* pp. 163-168.

Waller, S., & Lorch, B. (1977). First drinking experiences and present drinking patterns: A male-female comparison. *American Journal of Drug and Alcohol Abuse, 4,* pp. 109-121.

Wechsler, H., & McFadden, M. (1976). Sex differences in adolescent alcohol and drug use: A disappearing phenomenon. *Journal of Studies on Alcohol, 37:* pp. 1291-1301.

Wechsler, H., & McFadden, M. (1979). Drinking among college students in New England. *Journal of Studies on Alcohol, 40(11),* pp. 969-996.

Wechsler, H., & Rohman, M. (1981). Extensive users of alcohol among college students. *Journal of Studies on Alcohol, 42*, pp. 149-155.

Wilsnack, R.W., & Wilsnack, S.C. (1978). Sex roles and drinking among adolescent girls. *Journal of Studies on Alcohol, 39*, pp. 1855-1874.

Windham, G.E., & Aldridge, M. (1965). *The use of beverage alcohol by adults in two Mississippi communities.* State College, Mississippi: Social Science Research Center, Mississippi State University.

Chapter 5
Current Issues in Effective Alcohol Education Programming

Alan D. Berkowitz and H. Wesley Perkins

This chapter evaluates the theoretical and empirical evidence for alcohol program effectiveness by reviewing strategies associated with two models of educational programming and suggests ways in which alcohol survey results can be used to promote the goals of each model. It concludes with a review of some methodological issues in the evaluation of alcohol education programs and makes suggestions for integrating alcohol abuse prevention with other health-related prevention activities.

Alcohol education programs designed to prevent alcohol abuse exist on the majority of college campuses in this country (Anderson & Gadaleto, 1985). Extensive research during the past decade on collegiate drinking problems documents the need for such programs, with most studies reporting problem drinking rates of about 20-25% in college populations (Berkowitz & Perkins, 1986a). In addition to creating and enforcing alcohol-use policies and regulating on-campus consumption, the majority of programs employ a traditional approach conveying legal and pharmacological information about alcohol and its physical and psychological effects.

Underlying these programs is the assumption that increased awareness of the effects of alcohol will result in attitudinal changes that will subsequently translate into behavioral changes. Yet, while a variety of educational programs have proven effective in increasing awareness and, to a lesser extent, in improving attitudes about alcohol use, these cognitive changes have seldom resulted in positive behavioral changes, as documented by several recent literature reviews of program effectiveness among youth in general (cf. Braucht & Braucht, 1984; Hanson, 1982; Kinder, Pape & Walfish, 1980) and among college students in particular (Oblander, 1984). These reviews call into question the assumption that imparting information necessarily leads to rational behavior based on that information.

The paucity of evidence for positive program outcomes does not necessarily mean that alcohol education programs are entirely ineffective. Literature reviews by Goodstadt and Caleekal-John (1984) and Oblander (1984) have suggested that significant behavioral changes may result from programs that include field or laboratory experience, are more intensive (involve greater commitment over an extended period of time), or are targeted to specific populations. Other programs with comprehensive prevention strategies that take into consideration the psychosocial influences on alcohol use (discussed below) may also provide reason for some degree of cautious optimism in the search for more effective programs. Finally, the apparent lack of program effectiveness may be partly a reflection of inadequacies in evaluation strategies used to assess changes in alcohol use patterns.

Models for Alcohol Abuse Prevention Programs

The division of prevention activities into primary, secondary, and tertiary can be used to describe various traditional and innovative alcohol education programming efforts (Dean, 1982a; Kinney & Peltier, 1986; Kraft, 1979). Summarized briefly, primary prevention employs community-wide interventions to reduce the chances that an individual will develop a problem. Secondary prevention focuses on early identification and treatment of individuals at risk for developing a problem or persons having a problem in its early stages. Tertiary prevention assists those with a problem in its more advanced stages.

Traditional approaches to alcohol abuse prevention concentrate on changing individual awareness or attitudes and on developing policies to regulate alcohol consumption. For example, primary prevention activities may include programs about the effects of excessive alcohol consumption (these may be presented during new student orientation or dormitory meetings) and the development of policies to limit locations and times that alcohol is provided. Secondary prevention activities include the training of students and staff in the identification and referral of potential problem drinkers, as well as the provision of special educational programs for groups exhibiting high alcohol use or at risk for alcohol problems. Tertiary prevention, the most common element in college programs, typically includes required or self-initiated individual counseling with health center staff.

Program administrators and educators have increasingly recognized the limited effectiveness of traditional approaches. Recently, more innovative, comprehensive strategies have emerged that give particular emphasis to peer influences on drinking. Research has consistently shown that peers provide the strongest and most pervasive influences on adolescent and young adult drinking. These peer influences outweigh the effects of personality, family, social background, and other aspects of an individual's environment (Kandel, 1980). The development of individual drinking patterns both prior to and during college takes place in the context of norms for alcohol use established and maintained within immediate peer groups. Alcohol education programs should therefore incorporate an appropriate emphasis on the relationship of individual drinking styles to peer norms. Thus, attempts to change alcohol-use patterns among college students should take into account these social-psychological influences and employ intervention strategies capable of encouraging change within and through peer networks.

Accordingly, some educators and researchers have developed peer-oriented strategies that consider the "social ecology" of the campus situation (Mills, Neal, & Peed-Neal, 1983; Perkins & Berkowitz, 1986a). Within this approach, peers are viewed as highly influential in the development of an individual's alcohol abuse problem or, alternatively, as individuals who can promote responsible alcohol use. Insofar as the campus environment may be perceived as encouraging or discouraging particular alcohol-related behavior, its role in enabling alcohol abuse must also be considered. A social ecology approach to alcohol education would channel peer influences toward the creation of a social environment where alcohol abuse is discouraged or alcohol abusers are referred for treatment; alcohol counseling would incorporate an understanding of peer dynamics and use group approaches.

An expanded orientation to the prevention of alcohol abuse can be introduced at all levels of the prevention model. Primary prevention strategies focusing on peer norms and networks have been explored the least, yet they may hold significant opportunities for limiting problem drinking in peer-intensive environments (such as most college campuses). Strategies that can be used to reduce perceived peer pressure to drink heavily include promoting social events that give greater visibility to peer moderation in alcohol use and publicizing the fact that most students already possess moderate, responsible alcohol-use attitudes (Perkins & Berkowitz, 1986a, 1986b). The establishment of support groups on campuses for children of alcoholics is an example of a peer-oriented secondary prevention technique that has grown in popularity. Here, students who are at higher risk for developing patterns of alcohol abuse can discuss problems in a context of mutual understanding and can build a supportive friendship network that might buffer the influences of wider, more permissive social norms and peer pressures. Group counseling sessions for alcohol abusers provide an obvious example of tertiary prevention.

The traditional and social ecology models of alcohol education are illustrated in Table 5.1, which presents examples of intervention strategies for each level of prevention. In practice, the six categories are not entirely discrete and may overlap, but they are distinguished here to clarify the variety of approaches that can be used.

The use of student paraprofessionals to provide alcohol education services is an example of overlap between the two mod-

Table 5.1
Alcohol Education Program Interventions

Level of Prevention	Traditional Model (Individual Knowledge/Attitude Change and Policy Restraints)	Social Ecology Model (Psychosocial Peer-Influenced Changes)
Primary (Target: entire campus)	Present information about program services and physical and psychological effects of alcohol use. Restrict use of alcohol in social spaces, prohibit use on campus, or require alternative beverages and food where alcohol is served.	Correct misperceptions of alcohol-use norms. Promote social events that give greater visibility to peer moderation.
Secondary (Target: individuals at risk for, or developing, alcohol problems)	Train peers in early identification of problem drinking. Require informational workshops for individuals referred from campus judicial system.	Provide peer role models for responsible alcohol use. Provide alternative peer/social environments for at-risk individuals. Confront issues of group enabling in communal situations (fraternities, dormitories, athletic teams, clubs).
Tertiary (Target: problem drinkers)	Required or self-initiated individual counseling.	Group counseling focusing on interpersonal processes.

els. Approximately 70% of the campuses surveyed by Anderson and Gadaleto (1985) train resident advisors or other students to help peers with drinking problems. These students function within a traditional model to provide information and identify potential problem drinkers. As peers who interact with and offer positive role models for others, these same students also operate within a social ecology model. Thus, in practice, the social ecology approach can use strategies already developed in more traditional programs.

The Use of Alcohol Surveys in Prevention Programs

Alcohol surveys can be integrated into all three levels of prevention within both a traditional and expanded social ecology model (see Table 5.2). Within the traditional model, surveys are valuable as needs assessment tools, and survey results can help tailor program activities. Many programs emphasize the importance of using surveys for these purposes (Upcraft & Eck, 1986). Within the social ecology model, alcohol survey results can be used to promote prevention efforts by identifying and correcting community-wide misperceptions regarding alcohol use on campus. For example, they can be used to present immediate feedback to students about their own behavior, which may be more interesting and more effective in promoting conscientious reflection than the presentation of factual, impersonal information about alcohol abuse. In practice, however, only a minority of institutions use alcohol surveys in conjunction with other program activities—less than half of the campuses sampled by Anderson and Gadaleto (1985) between 1983 and 1985 reported surveying student behaviors in relation to alcohol use—although Gonzalez (1986) has included research and evaluation as one of nine components of a model alcohol education program.

Some recently developed alcohol education programs use alcohol surveys in a manner consistent with a social ecology model. They incorporate strategies derived from a traditional model but expanded to include an emphasis on peer relationships and the psychosocial variables associated with alcohol use. In the "problem-specific approach" of Mills, et al. (1983), the entire campus community is involved in addressing alcohol-related problems that are identified through alcohol surveys. Efforts of alcohol education programs focus on developing solutions to these problems and rely on grassroots community sup-

Table 5.2
Use of Alcohol Surveys in Alcohol Education Programs

Level of Prevention	Traditional Model (Needs Assessment)	Social Ecology Model (Integration of Peer Results)
Primary	Determine level of student knowledge of alcohol effects in order to develop programs, curricula, etc., to provide needed information.	Identify community-wide norms regarding alcohol use and expose widely held misperceptions.
Secondary	Identify groups of individuals at risk for problem drinking (e.g., children of alcoholics) and determine size of group and extent of problem.	Reveal misperceptions about alcohol-use patterns and attitudes of problem-prone groups to their own membership (e.g., fraternities).
	Identify the different patterns of alcohol abuse in specific groups, and tailor programs and workshops accordingly.	Utilize alcohol survey results to create group discussion, and reinforce existing moderate norms within particular social groups.
Tertiary	Identify size and nature of subpopulation requiring counseling services.	Utilize survey data to help clients assess themselves more accurately in the context of the large community.

port for change. Thus, in the "problem-specific approach," peer educators serve as catalysts for changing alcohol-related problems identified through campus surveys rather than merely providing general information to individuals about alcohol and its effects.

In our campus program, we have included a social ecology approach that relies on the extensive use of ongoing survey research (Perkins & Berkowitz, 1986b). In primary prevention activities, we have presented students with survey results revealing that most students actually hold moderate personal attitudes toward alcohol use but misperceive their peers as being much more liberal (Perkins & Berkowitz, 1986a, 1986b). This is an important concern because widespread misperceptions regarding campus-wide drinking attitudes can influence the contexts in which students drink and the amounts they consume. Correcting these misperceptions through the presentation of alcohol survey data in campus symposia, newspapers, and dormitory discussions may provide a means of positively influencing student alcohol use patterns on campus. A reduction in misperceptions of peers as extremely liberal might encourage a shift away from heavy personal drinking for some individuals, especially in public settings. As a result, students may be even less likely to perceive the campus drinking environment as liberal, and thus be encouraged to adopt greater moderation in alcohol use. This trend may initiate a snowball effect involving a mutually reinforcing sequence of more accurate perceptions coupled with greater moderation in public drinking behavior.

It is useful to identify specific groups of students that can be targeted for secondary prevention. Programs can be designed to focus intervention efforts on critical transition periods (Winick, 1985). For example, our alcohol surveys have identified the first year of college as the transition period when the greatest changes in alcohol consumption occur (Berkowitz & Perkins, 1985a). Survey data can also be used to tailor programs to meet the needs of particular groups of students (Perkins & Berkowitz, 1986a). In our research, we have identified distinctive patterns of alcohol use among students living in fraternities (Perkins & Berkowitz, 1986a), students who are children from alcohol-abusing families (Berkowitz & Perkins, 1985b), students from different religious backgrounds (Perkins, 1985; Perkins, 1987), and between male and female students (Berkowitz & Perkins, 1985a; Berkowitz & Perkins, 1987). These patterns can be used to develop specific educational strategies within the framework of a traditional approach. Within a social ecology model, alcohol survey results can be used to reveal misperceptions about alcohol use patterns and attitudes within problem-prone groups.

For example, in fraternity alcohol awareness programs, we have used survey results to examine fraternity drinking patterns, explore campus myths about fraternity drinking, and identify misperceptions held by fraternity members about their own alcohol use (Perkins & Berkowitz, 1986a).

In tertiary prevention, alcohol surveys can be used to assess the size and nature of subpopulations requiring counseling (traditional model). Surveys also have applications in individual and group counseling sessions, where clients can evaluate themselves in the context of accurate data on campus-wide patterns of alcohol use (social ecology model).

Alcohol Education in Relation to Other Prevention Programs

Researchers have called attention to the fact that abuse is related to other problem behaviors, such as drug abuse, precocious sexual behavior, delinquency (Braucht & Braucht, 1984), or eating disorders (Claydon, 1986). These patterns suggest that alcohol education approaches could be integrated within the broader context of health promotion activities. Thus, services can be combined for children from a variety of problem or abusing families (for instance, involving physical or sexual abuse, or other addictions such as compulsive gambling) that have similar emotional consequences to family alcoholism. Counselors treating students for one of these difficulties should be aware of the potential overlap in problem areas among these students. Similarly, presentations focusing on alcohol use can be expanded to explore the relationship of alcohol to other health concerns, such as sexuality, drug use, and nutrition. Thus, issues surrounding alcohol use or the effects of its abuse can be explored within a larger context relating to other health issues and/ or problem behaviors.

Issues in Program Evaluations

Ultimately, any program must face the question: Does it work or is it successful in achieving its goals? The answer to this question depends not only upon whether desired changes are taking place but also upon how we define and measure those changes.

Thus, a number of issues are encountered in the evaluation process, including defining effectiveness, sampling target groups appropriately, and designing strategies for adequately assessing change. The previously reported ineffectiveness of most alcohol education programs in promoting positive behavioral changes may, in part, be due to inadequate attention to these methodological issues.

Defining effectiveness. Determining the effectiveness of a program presupposes clearly articulated goals for particular prevention activities as well as for the program as a whole. Yet, a problem plaguing many outcome studies is the lack of a comprehensive theoretical framework within which goals can be conceptualized and the subsequent lack of clearly operationalized variables for measuring change. For example, the decision about whether one seeks to measure change in terms of knowledge, attitudes, or behaviors involves assumptions about the primary problem and about program goals that need to be articulated and that may vary depending upon the characteristics of the target group.

The concept of problem drinking itself provides an example of the complexity involved in selecting particular measures (Berkowitz & Perkins, 1986a). In a recent study of college students, different measures of problem drinking—heavy consumption, frequent negative consequences, negative drinking motivations, frequent intoxication, and self-identification as a problem drinker—showed only a modest empirical overlap, and prevalence rates for each measure varied differently among various student groups (Perkins & Berkowitz, 1985).

A measurement instrument that explores a broad range of alcohol-related phenomena may be most useful for the comprehensive assessment of program effects. Claydon and Johnson (1985) recently described the development of such a survey instrument (including item reliability and validity assessments). It provides measurements of alcohol-related knowledge, attitudes, and behaviors, as well as important demographic variables. The survey can be used for specific subpopulations or for the entire student community. Given the research reviewed earlier on the relationship of misperceptions to drinking patterns, however, it may also be important to include measures of perceived variables in future studies. Furthermore, it is important to include survey measures of students' awareness of and participation in alcohol program activities available on campus. If one finds, for example, that there has been little change in a measure of problem drinking among students, one must be able to distinguish whether the general lack of effect is due to lack of student exposure or to a strategy that is ineffective when it has reached students.

Evaluating effectiveness also requires distinguishing the performance of individuals or groups responsible for delivering program services from the outcome of interventions that have been provided. That is, failure of a program to produce positive changes may be due to poor execution of a strategy rather than the strategy itself. With regard to program performance, for example, we found that resident advisors on our campus were acting as appropriate role models in terms of their relatively moderate consumption levels, their awareness of program services, and their referral of alcohol abusers for treatment, but not with respect to their incurring negative consequences resulting from their own alcohol use and their perceptions of campus alcohol norms (Berkowitz & Perkins, 1986b).

Sampling issues. Appropriate selection of the group to be evaluated is extremely important. Evaluations may focus on change in an entire campus population or in a smaller group of individuals within a community (such as members of a living unit or recipients of a particular service). On the one hand, since different interventions may vary in their effectiveness among specific groups of students, assessing the average effect of a single intervention among all students may camouflage or dilute significant program effects that exist only in particular constituencies (Braucht & Braucht, 1984). On the other hand, another problem may occur when focusing exclusively on results of specific, individual interventions in particular groups rather than on what might be a significant cumulative effect of the entire range of services and outreach activities offered. That is, significant changes may occur only among students who are exposed to multiple interventions that mutually reinforce each other, producing an interaction effect. Thus, collecting samples from the general population in which some students may have multiple program experiences is as important as collecting data from specific target groups. Well-designed evaluations will, therefore, typically need to accomplish two objectives: assess the impact of specific interventions on particular groups of students and at the same time evaluate the cumulative effect of multiple interventions on individual students and on the campus as a whole.

Evaluation samples should be clear representatives of the target group for whom program effects are desired. Thus, for example, it may not be accurate to measure changes in alcohol-use patterns by asking administrators about their perceptions of students. Furthermore, students who participate in alcohol education program activities may not always be representative of students at large. One way of avoiding this problem is to draw a sample from all members of a particular community, living unit, or target group, although this may not always be practical. If not, then adequate procedures for obtaining a randomized representative sample are essential.

Strategies for assessing change. The problem of designing a strategy that distinguishes program effects from other influences remains, even when all of the above-mentioned concerns regarding program goal definition, implementation measurement, and sampling have been addressed. A few of the primary concerns will be described.

In the traditional experimental design model, one group is administered a "treatment" (e.g., exposure to a workshop or a particular counseling technique) and is then compared with a control group not exposed to it. Although this is perhaps the most common evaluation strategy for isolating treatment effects, it has a number of limitations. Besides the common problem of establishing initial comparability between the treatment and control groups, one faces the question of the validity and generalizability of results when self-selected samples have been employed (as has often been the case in alcohol education programs). Furthermore, this approach is usually limited to evaluating specific interventions and thus excludes any evaluation of comprehensive program effects.

Researchers may avoid some of these problems by surveying a randomly selected representative sample of a target population before, or at the beginning of, a new alcohol program and then surveying another random sample after the program has been in existence for some time, especially if the sample sizes are large and the data is collected anonymously. Other cautions must be observed with this approach. Most problematic is the occurrence of historical changes in the social situation (e.g., a change in the legal drinking age or in the cost of alcoholic beverages) that might influence alcohol use and thus confound the interpretation of any differences observed in data from the two surveys.

Timing provides another concern. Evaluation data collected shortly after program exposure are not particularly reliable for determining meaningful change in attitudes and behaviors. Initial differences that might appear may be due to temporary reactions that do not persist as lasting attitudinal or behavioral changes. Alternatively, an alcohol program may require an extended period of time to gain attention or fully influence its participants. Thus, significant effects may not appear in an immediate follow-up study. However, for both small experiments and large surveys, evaluations are also problematic if they are conducted after a substantial length of time. Experimental- and control-groups samples that are initially small can suffer significant attrition over a lengthy time period, thus rendering the results of a comparison meaningless. Extending the period of time between large representative surveys increases the likelihood of confounding historical changes occurring between the two samplings.

Conclusion

We recommend that alcohol education programs include activities consistent with a social ecology approach while integrating alcohol survey research into program activities. In addition, student affairs staff and alcohol education program administrators in particular need to pay more attention to the clarification of theoretical premises that underlie their efforts and to more adequate evaluation of program effectiveness.

It is important that alcohol education programming be expanded to encompass activities within all three levels of prevention. Dean (1982b), Kinney and Peltier (1986), and Wilsnack and Wilsnack (1982) have commented on the need for systematic program efforts that incorporate a wide range of prevention strategies. A well-planned program that integrates activities within all six areas of prevention (see Table 5.1) will be able to reach and involve a greater number of individuals. Thus, programs limited to tertiary or secondary activities need an expanded emphasis including primary, community-wide interventions, while traditional programs in general need a broader framework incorporating the perspectives of a social ecology model.

As part of the development of more comprehensive programs, alcohol surveys can be effectively employed in the design and delivery of services at all prevention levels as well as in programs. Monitoring programs through evaluation instruments can provide valuable feedback, which can be used to help shape ongoing programs, to program administrators. The value of these evaluations is determined, however, by the degree of attention given to the methodological concerns that have been discussed here.

In addition, the intensity and continuity of prevention efforts should be increased. Programs requiring continuing involvement over time can be more effective than single interventions at only one point in time. There is also evidence that tailoring programs to meet the specific needs of particular groups of students is equally as important as offering generalized programs to larger audiences. Ultimately, the cumulative impact of expanding program efforts in all of the above areas may be to generate the critical mass necessary to produce individual and community change in alcohol-use attitudes, behaviors, and norms.

* * * * *

(The authors gratefully acknowledge the assistance of the Christopher D. Smithers Foundation in their research.)

References

Anderson, D.S., & Gadaleto, A.F. (1985, October). *Results of the 1979, 1982 and 1985 college alcohol survey.* Paper presented at the National Collegiate Alcohol Awareness Week Conference, New York University.

Berkowitz, A.D., & Perkins, H.W. (1985a, March). *Gender differences in collegiate drinking: Longitudinal trends and developmental patterns.* Paper presented at the Annual Meeting of the American College Personnel Association, Boston, MA.

Berkowitz, A.D., & Perkins, H.W. (1985b, May/June). *Children from alcohol abusing families as college students: Their drinking patterns and problems.* Paper presented at the Annual Meeting of the American College Health Association, Washington, DC.

Berkowitz, A.D., & Perkins, H.W. (1986a). Problem drinking among college students: A review of recent research. *Journal of American College Health, 35*(1), pp. 21-28.

Berkowitz, A.D., & Perkins, H.W. (1986b). Resident advisors as role models: a comparison of resident advisor and student peer drinking patterns. *Journal of College Student Personnel, 27*(2), pp. 146-153.

Berkowitz, A.D., & Perkins, H.W. (1987). Recent research on gender differences in collegiate alcohol use. *Journal of American College Health, 35*, p. 5.

Braucht, N.B., & Braucht, B. (1984). Prevention of problem drinking among youth: Evaluation of educational strategies. In P.M. Miller & T.D. Nerenberg (Eds.), *Prevention of alcohol abuse.* New York: Plenum Press.

Claydon, P.D. (1986, April). *Self reported alcohol/drug and eating disorder problems among entering freshmen with parental alcoholism: A preliminary study.* Paper presented at the Third National Conference on Alcohol and Drug Abuse Issues in Higher Education, San Antonio, TX.

Claydon, P.D., & Johnson, M.E. (1985). An instrument for needs assessment and evaluation of alcohol education programs: The Claydon college drinking questionnaire. *Journal of Alcohol and Drug Education, 31*, pp. 41-50.

Dean, J.C. (1982a). Alcohol programming: A conceptual model. In J.C. Dean & W.A. Bryan (Eds.), *Alcohol programming for higher education* (pp. 15-29). Carbondale: Southern Illinois University Press.

Dean, J.C. (1982b). Approaches to alcohol abuse prevention. In J.C. Dean & W.A. Bryan (Eds.), *Alcohol programming for higher education* (pp. 30-43). Carbondale: Southern Illinois University Press.

Gonzalez, G. (1986). Proactive efforts and selected alcohol education programs. In T.G. Goodale (Ed.), *Alcohol and the college student* (pp. 17-34). San Francisco: Jossey-Bass.

Goodstadt, M.S., & Caleekal-John, A. (1984). Alcohol education programs for university students: A review of their effectiveness. *The International Journal of the Addictions, 19,* pp. 721-741.

Hanson, D.J. (1982). The effectiveness of alcohol and drug education. *Journal of Alcohol and Drug Education, 27,* pp. 1-13.

Kandel, D.B. (1980). Drug and drinking behavior among youth. In A. Inkles, N.J. Smelser, & R. Turner (Eds.), *Annual review of sociology, 6* (pp. 235-285). Palo Alto, CA: Annual Reviews, Inc.

Kinder, B.N., Pape, E., & Walfish, S. (1980). Drug and alcohol education programs: A review of outcome studies. *The International Journal of the Addictions, 15,* pp. 1035-1054.

Kinney, J., & Peltier, D. (1986). A model alcohol program for the college health service. *Journal of American College Health, 34,* pp. 229-233.

Kraft, D.P. (1979). Strategies for reducing drinking problems among youth: college programs. In H.T. Blane & M.E. Chafez (Eds.), *Youth, alcohol and social policy* (pp. 311-354). New York: Plenum Press.

Mills, K.C., Neal, M.N., & Peed-Neal, I. (1983). *A handbook for alcohol education: The community approach.* Cambridge, MA: Ballinger Publishing Company.

Oblander, F.W. (1984). A practice oriented synthesis: Effective alcohol education strategies. *ACU-I Bulletin,* (October), pp. 17-23.

Perkins, H.W. (1985). Religious traditions, parents and peers as determinants of alcohol and drug use among college students. *Review of Religious Research, 27,* pp. 15-31.

Perkins, H.W. (1987, September). Parental religion and alcohol use problems as intergenerational predictors of problem-drinking among college youth. Forthcoming in *Journal for the Scientific Study of Religion*, Vol 26, #3.

Perkins, H.W., & Berkowitz, A.D. (1985, August). *Conceptual and methodological difficulties in defining problem drinking among college students: Research findings from an extensive campus survey.* Paper presented at the Annual Meeting of the American College Health Association, Washington, DC.

Perkins, H.W., & Berkowitz, A.D. (1986a). Perceiving the community norms of alcohol use among students: Some research implications for campus alcohol education programming. *The International Journal of the Addictions, 21* (9/10), pp. 961-976.

Perkins, H.W., & Berkowitz, A.D. (1986b). Using student alcohol surveys: Notes on clinical and educational program applications. *Journal of Alcohol and Drug Education, 31*(2), pp. 44-51.

Upcraft, M.L., & Eck, W.E. (1986). In T.G. Goodale (Ed.), *Alcohol and the college student* (pp. 35-42). San Francisco: Jossey-Bass.

Wilsnack, R.W., & Wilsnack, S.C. (1982). Introduction and overview. In J.C. Dean & W.A. Bryan, (Eds.), *Alcohol programming for higher education* (pp. 1-4). Carbondale: Southern Illinois University Press.

Winick, C. (1985). Specific targeting of prevention programs in alcohol and drug dependence. *The International Journal of the Addictions, 20*, pp. 527-533.

Chapter 6

Alcohol Policy Development: A Necessary Component for a Comprehensive Alcohol Education Program on Campus

Gerardo M. Gonzalez

Americans are becoming increasingly health conscious (Taylor, 1984). Along with their concern for health and wellness, they are also exercising a greater degree of moderation in their use of alcoholic beverages. These trends are also in evidence on the college campus. However, there still is a high incidence of alcohol-related problems on campus. Moreover, alcohol education programs designed to address these problems remain in need of a theoretical base, greater allocation of program resources, and acceptance as an integral part of the institution's mission, policies, and services.

The purpose of this chapter is to accentuate the importance of alcohol policy development as an integral part of a comprehensive campus alcohol education and prevention program. Further, the chapter provides a methodology for campus policy development that is based on sound theoretical principles and practical campus realities.

The Public Health Model

In order to develop a theoretical base for alcohol education programs in colleges, educators must begin by taking a broader look at alcohol education than has been the case traditionally. The public health model of prevention offers a useful theoretical framework to accomplish this objective. According to public health principles, problems are seen as stemming from an interaction among three factors: the host, the agent, and the environment (Noble, 1978). Intervention at any or all of these points is appropriate for the prevention of alcohol problems on campus. The three key elements of this model are (a) the host—the individual and his or her biopsychosocial susceptibilities to alcohol problems as well as the individual's knowledge about alcohol, attitudes that influence drinking patterns, and drinking behavior itself; (b) the agent—characteristics, availability, specific chemistry, and effects of alcohol; and (c) the environment—the setting or context in which drinking occurs; the campus and community mores that shape drinking practices; and the legal sanctions, controls, and policy regulations that govern alcohol use on campus.

All three elements of the public health model are interactive and interdependent. Thus, in approaching the prevention of alcohol problems on campus, the most effective strategies would be those that deal with all three elements of the public health model. Gains made in any one area will positively affect the other two areas. Boswell and Boswell (1984) point out that by employing the public health model, prevention programs can both expand opportunities for health promotion and create a shared forum of understanding.

The historical perspective presented by Joseph M. Fischer in Chapter 1 shows that, in the past, most campus alcohol abuse prevention programs have focused exclusively on the individual student. However, more recently, colleges have begun to examine their alcohol policies and many have revised them to be more consistent with the alcohol education messages that have been directed at students over the years. Results of a BACCHUS survey of chief student affairs officers (Gonzalez & Broughton, 1986) in cooperation with the National Association of Student Personnel Administrators during the spring term of 1985, showed that 54% of the schools surveyed had revised their alcohol policies within a two-year period preceding the survey. A review of the policies submitted with the questionnaire indicated that campus alcohol policies are becoming more comprehensive in nature and often include requirements that social events on campus be registered prior to their scheduled times, that such events adhere to certain predetermined guidelines such as providing nonalcoholic beverages, and that advertising for the events not feature alcohol as their main focus.

Several studies and reports document the growing rate and development of alcohol education programs in higher education (Anderson & Gadaleto, 1985; Becker, Wanner, & White, 1983; Ingalls, 1982). Moreover, as Caryl K. Smith points out in Chapter 3, largely because of the federal legislation threatening states with a loss of highway funds if they do not raise their drinking age to 21 by October 1986, increasing numbers of colleges are revising their alcohol policies (Connell, 1985; Fiske, 1983; Ingalls, 1983; *Newsweek on Campus*, 1985). By revising their alcohol policies, the colleges are, in effect, changing the contextual environment where drinking takes place on campus. Most of the new policies are incorporating into their texts the principles long advocated in alcohol education programs for party planning, student assistance intervention, alcohol-related training, health promotion, and other areas. Further, there is increasing evidence that the top echelons of institutional governance are getting more involved in the formulation of alcohol policy on campus (Connor, 1985; Gonzalez, 1985).

Evidently, because of the discussion concerning proper standards of behavior related to drinking that the alcohol education programs have generated on campus, a consensus has begun to emerge about acceptable standards of alcohol-related behavior within the institutions. And there is a growing willingness among the colleges to articulate, in the form of written policies, what those standards are. Thus, a new alcohol abuse prevention strategy that is focused on changing the drinking environment is emerging on campus. It is likely that these trends will enhance the alcohol education activities and improve the social context in which drinking occurs. Moreover, formulation of comprehensive and enforceable alcohol policies might provide the institutions with the best protection against the growing threat of legal liability in alcohol-related cases.

Legal Liability Issues

Increasingly, court rulings are making it clear that, in addition to a moral duty to provide students with safe campus environments, colleges have a financial stake in taking precautions to prevent abusive drinking on campus. The case *Bradshaw v. Rawlings*, involving Delaware Valley College, in which an appeals court overturned a decision that the institution was liable for injuries to a student returning from a sophomore picnic at which beer was served, established that although colleges do not have a duty to control the behavior of students, they do have a duty to care. And that "duty to care" requires colleges to provide due warning where there is a clear and present danger and to ensure that the institution's activities, offerings, and programs meet minimum standards of care for its students. According to the white paper prepared for the American Council on Education by Gulland and Flournoy (1985), and discussed by Mary Lou Fenili in Chapter 2, tort liability is routinely imposed in hindsight on the basis of a jury's or judge's feeling that someone's breach of a "duty to care" has "proximately caused" the plaintiff's injury. The authors suggest that colleges and universities can minimize their exposure to tort liability by understanding the principal risks and dealing with their responsibilities. That does not simply mean promulgating strict rules; unrealistic rules that are incapable of practical enforcement can actually invite greater liability by defining a set of duties that schools do not and cannot satisfy. However, by acting knowledgeably and realistically, schools can provide strong evidence of their efforts to live up to the "duty to care" that may reasonably be demanded of them. Gulland and Flournoy recommend that every school appraise its alcohol policy in light of the changing temper of public policy toward alcohol abuse. Furthermore, they indicate that every college and university has a policy toward its students' use of alcohol. The policy consists of what the school really does about the issue, not necessarily what its written pronouncements say. Those schools that think they have no policy fail to realize that they actually have a policy of approaching the question in a less formal, more ad hoc manner.

A Model Alcohol Policy

In an effort to develop a model alcohol policy that could be modified and adopted by individual colleges, several national groups of college administrators established the Inter-Association Task Force on Alcohol Issues in 1982. Current participants in the Task Force include the American College Personnel Association, the National Association of Student Personnel Administrators, the Association of College Unions—International, the Association of College and University Housing Officers—International, the National Association for Campus Activities, the National Association of College and University Residence Halls, the National Orientation Directors Association, the National Interfraternity Conference, the United States Student Association, and BACCHUS—the college alcohol education program that began at the University of Florida in 1976 and that now has more than 200 campus chapters. BACCHUS stands for Boost Alcohol Consciousness Concerning the Health of University Students.

At a November 1984 meeting of the Inter-Association Task Force on Alcohol Issues, members approved a "Model Alcohol Policy" statement for colleges that permits the possession, consumption, or serving of alcoholic beverages. This "Model Policy" was first published by Gonzalez (1985) in *AGB Reports*, a publication of the Association of Governing Boards of Colleges and Universities. The statement is designed to help colleges develop or revise alcohol policies to conform to reasonable standards of care.

Many experts believe that a governing board-approved, comprehensive alcohol policy is necessary as a risk management tool for colleges and universities. Moreover experts believe that a sound alcohol policy, instead of establishing a custodial relationship with students, should be based on the concepts of freedom of choice and responsibility that legal adults are entitled to in our society and that have long been a part of the higher education tradition. The Task Force incorporated these principles into its guidelines for a model alcohol policy, which can be found in the Appendix.

The Task Force also recommended that active alcohol programs be established to meet the institution's obligation of providing due warning. Such programs should inform students about the danger of excessive drinking and proper ways to reduce personal risk related to alcohol use.

Perhaps the greatest mistake a college can make in response to the 21-as-drinking-age legislation or the legal liability issue is to ban alcohol on campus and then look the other way. A reasonable and realistic balance between the educational mission and the enforcement responsibilities of the institution must be sought. As Tom Goodale points out in the Introduction, "while rules and regulations are important and necessary, the reduction of problems related to the misuse of alcohol cannot be achieved solely through the development of rules and regulations; students must be educated about the principles behind the policies." Educational leaders everywhere need to face the challenge that alcohol abuse poses to colleges and universities and to let reason prevail on the controversial and emotional issue of drinking on campus.

Implementation of Model Policy

The policy model outlined above is not intended to be an edict; rather, it is a guide. It can provide the starting point for policy discussions on a particular campus. Once a decision is made on a campus to review its alcohol policy, the Inter-Association policy model can be used to start the process. The most effective way to revise and adopt a new alcohol policy is for the college president or a senior vice president to appoint a committee to draft and make recommendations concerning what the new policy should be. Each member of the committee can then be given a copy of the Inter-Association model policy for review and discussion at the first committee meeting.

The makeup of the alcohol policy committee is a very important aspect of the policy development project. The committee should include both campus and community representatives. As a minimum, campus representation should include the chief student affairs officer, the chief counsel for the university, the student body president, the editor of the campus newspaper, campus security personnel, members of the faculty, athletic association personnel, housing personnel, and other appropriate groups. Representatives from the community might include the following: a local alcohol distributor; local law-enforcement personnel; a local politician; a local media person; and representatives from the local council of churches, a local insurance company, and the chamber of commerce.

However creative a campus administrator is in selecting representatives for the university committee, the committee must not be a rubber stamp; it must be active, cooperative, and a reflection of the community and campus interests. Its individuals must be able to speak officially for their constituencies.

Once all the members of the university's committee are chosen and regular committee meetings are set, a schedule of research and support activities should be assigned to each committee member. Drs. Engs and Hanson, in Chapter 4, as well as Drs. Berkowitz and Perkins in Chapter 5, have discussed the importance of research. This kind of data collection and participation is essential to the project. The college administration has now shared the responsibility, and the constituent representatives are committed and involved in promoting their own interests and concerns within guidelines that are acceptable and beneficial to the university and its students.

The committee is then charged with reviewing the Inter-Association Task Force policy model as a step-by-step guide in developing a policy specific to that particular campus and community. The Inter-Association model may fit exactly, or the committee may need to create replacements or additions. The resultant campus policy should then be submitted by each representative to his or her organization for its official approval. That approval should be incorporated into the documentation of the university's policy initiative.

A policy with broad, professional authorship carries much more credibility in risk management and legal issues than a policy narrowly formulated to fit only campus administration perspectives and interests. After all the input from the various groups has been received and incorporated into the final policy draft, the chairperson should forward the committee's recommendation to the president of the college for approval. The president should then seek approval by the highest governing body of the institution that has final authority and responsibility for the adoption of the new policy.

Once the policy is finalized and adopted, it should be widely disseminated and publicized within the campus and surrounding community. Communication of policy expectations should be an ongoing, year-round effort. Drs. Berkowitz and Perkins reminded us in Chapter 5 of the importance of perceived expectations for drinking behavior on campus. Only when the community and the students become aware of and understand the principles and practical realities behind the policy can compliance be expected. Moreover, widespread understanding and support for the policy will facilitate consistent and fair enforcement over time. Such understanding and support can be obtained only through a comprehensive and sustained alcohol education program on campus—one that is based on a sound, positive philosophy; is backed by a serious institutional commitment to its success; and involves students as an integral, active part of the educational process. In short, an alcohol education program that answers in the affirmative the first question posed by Dr. Goodale in the Introduction: Does it go as far as it can?

References

Anderson, D.S., & Gadaleto, A.F. (1985, March). *That happy feeling: An alcohol education overview and report on national sur-*

veys. Paper presented at the American College Personnel Association Conference, Boston, MA.

Becker, N., Wanner, C., & White, J. (1983). Alcohol on American campuses: A directory of programs, a survey of American colleges and a model student assistance program. *Policy Perspectives*, 3(3), pp. 1-103.

Boswell, B.N., & Boswell, R.H. (1984, August). *Participate prevention*. Paper presented at the 35th Annual Conference of the Alcohol and Drug Problems Association, Washington, DC.

Connell, C. (1985, January/February). Drinking on campus—The 21-year-old drinking age: education or enforcement? *CHANGE*, p. 44.

Connor, J.R. (1985). *Report of the university of Wisconsin system advisory committee on alcohol education.* Madison: The University of Wisconsin System.

Fiske, E.B. (1983, March 8). Colleges press alcohol curbs as states raise drinking age. *The New York Times*, p. 1.

Gonzalez, G.M. (1985). Alcohol on campus: You must insure its responsible use. *AGB Reports*, 27(4), pp. 24-28.

Gonzalez, G.M., & Broughton, E.A. (1986). Status of alcohol policies on campus: A national survey. *NASPA Journal*, 24(2), pp. 49-59.

Gulland, E.E., & Flournoy, A.C. (1985). *Universities, colleges and alcohol: An overview of tort liability issues.* White Paper on Student Alcohol Abuse Prepared for the American Council on Education, Washington, DC.

Ingalls, Z. (1983, February 9). Campuses face changes in policies as states raise legal drinking age. *Chronicle of Higher Education*, p. 1.

Ingalls, Z. (1982, July 21). Higher education's drinking problem. *Chronicle of Higher Education*, p. 1.

A new publication. (1985, April). *Newsweek on Campus*, p. 7.

Noble, E.P. (Ed.). (1978). *Third Special Report to the U.S. Congress on Alcohol and Health.* Washington, DC: Superintendent of Public Documents, U.S. Government Printing Office.

Taylor, H. (1984, November). *Prevention in America II: Steps People Take—or Fail to Take—for Better Health, 1984.* New York: Louis Harris and Associates, Inc.

Appendix

Inter-Association Task Force
Model Campus Alcohol Policy Guidelines

The Task Force recommends that a comprehensive campus policy on alcohol include a summary of state and city laws covering each of the following areas:

1. Drinking Age Laws pertaining to the possession, consumption, and sale of alcoholic beverages as well as penalties for violation of such laws.
2. Regulations of Sale Laws with special emphasis on Alcohol Beverage Control (ABC) Board's requirements for special permits or licenses by groups that charge admission or dues for events involving alcoholic beverages.
3. Open Container Laws governed by city or county ordinances or state statutes concerning the consumption of alcoholic beverages in outdoor areas or automobiles.
4. Other Laws pertinent to the jurisdiction (such as dram shop or implied consent laws).

College Regulations

In addition to legal responsibilities, The Task Force recommends that the following regulations be instituted as part of an alcohol policy on campus:

1. Locations where alcoholic beverages are permitted to be possessed, served, and consumed by persons of legal drinking age on the campus should be visibly marked. A specific listing of such places (e.g., in private rooms, designated common areas of residence halls, college unions, etc.) helps clarify questions that students, faculty, or staff might have about where alcoholic beverages are permitted on campus.

2. Locations where alcoholic beverages are permitted to be sold as opposed to merely served on campus (e.g., faculty lounge, college union, pub, etc.) should be delineated clearly.

3. Guidelines should be established regarding public and private social events that involve alcoholic beverages within the institution's jurisdiction. An event that is open to the public (i.e., where admission is charged or public announcement is made) should be registered with the appropriate campus office before the event. Such events should be conducted within the following guidelines:

    a. If the function includes the sale of alcoholic beverages, a permit should be obtained from the appropriate state office or ABC Board.

    b. Individuals sponsoring the event should implement precautionary measures to ensure that alcoholic beverages are not accessible or served to persons under the legal drinking age or to persons who appear intoxicated.

    c. At social functions where alcoholic beverages are provided by the sponsoring organization, direct access should be limited to a person(s) designated as the server(s).

    d. Consumption of alcoholic beverages should be permitted only within the approved area designated for the event.

e. Nonalcoholic beverages must be available at the same place as the alcoholic beverages and featured as prominently as the alcoholic beverages.

f. A reasonable portion of the budget for the event shall be designated for the purchase of food items.

g. No social event shall include any form of "drinking contest" in its activities or promotion.

h. Advertisements for any university event at which alcoholic beverages are served shall mention the availability of nonalcoholic beverages as prominently as alcohol. Alcohol should not be used as an inducement to participate in a campus event.

i. Promotional materials including advertising for any university event shall not make reference to the amount of alcoholic beverages (such as number of beer kegs) available.

j. Institutionally approved security personnel shall be present at all times during the event.

4. A specific statement concerning the use or nonuse of alcoholic beverages at membership recruitment functions (e.g., fraternity/sorority rush, departmental clubs, and special interest groups) should be an integral part of a comprehensive campus alcohol policy.

5. A specific statement concerning the use or nonuse of alcoholic beverages in athletic facilities or at athletic events should be included as part of a comprehensive campus alcohol policy. Such a statement should apply equally to students, faculty, staff, alumni, and others attending the event.

6. Guidelines for any marketing, advertising, or promotion of alcoholic beverages on campus or at campus events involving alcohol should be stated as part of a comprehensive campus alcohol policy.

7. Procedures for adjudicating violations of the alcohol policy should be articulated. Such procedures should include an explicit statement of sanctions.